CONTENTS

D0019039

Why is our travel information the best in the world? It's simple: our authors are passionate, dedicated travellers. They don't take freebies in exchange for positive coverage so you can be sure the advice you're given is impartial. They travel widely to all the popular spots, and off the beaten track. They don't research using just the internet or phone. They discover new places not included in any other guidebook. They personally visit thousands of hotels, restaurants, palaces, trails, galleries, temples and more. They speak with dozens of locals every day to make sure you get the kind of insider knowledge only a local could tell you. They take pride in getting all the details right, and in telling it how it is. Think you can do it? Find out how at **lonelyplanet.com**.

BALI

ENCOUNTER

RYAN VER BERKMOES

Bali Encounter

Published by Lonely Planet Publications Pty Ltd
ABN 36 005 607 983

Australia	Head Office, Locked Bag 1,
	Footscray, Victoria 3011
	☎ 03 8379 8000 fax 03 8379 8111
	talk2us@lonelyplanet.com.au
USA	150 Linden St, Oakland, CA 94607
	☎ 510 250 6400
	toll free 800 275 8555
	fax 510 893 8572
	info@lonelyplanet.com
UK	2nd fl, 186 City Rd,
	London EC1V 2NT
	☎ 020 7106 2100 fax 020 7
	go@lonelyplanet.co.uk

This title was commissioned in Lonely Planet's
Melbourne office and produced by: **Commissio**
Editors Shawn Low, Ilaria Walker, Tashi Wheel
Coordinating Editor Nigel Chin **Cartographe**
Bogdanovits **Coordinating Layout Designer**
Managing Editors Bruce Evans, Liz Heynes **M**
Cartographer Corey Hutchison **Managing La**
Designer Celia Wood **Internal Image Resea**
Sabrina Dalbesio, lonelyplanetimages.com **Cove**
Researcher Naomi Parker, lonelyplanetimages.com
Thanks to Errol Hunt, Indra Kilfoyle, Lisa Knights

ISBN 978 1 74179 717 6

Printed by Hang Tai Printing Company, Hong Kong.
Printed in China.

Lonely Planet and the Lonely Planet logo are trademarks
of Lonely Planet and are registered in the US Patent and
Trademark Office and in other countries.

Lonely Planet does not allow its name or logo to be
appropriated by commercial establishments, such as
retailers, restaurants or hotels. Please let us know of any
misuses: www.lonelyplanet.com/ip.

HOW TO USE THIS BOOK
Colour-Coding & Maps
Colour-coding is used for symbols on maps and in
the text that they relate to (eg all eating venues on
the maps and in the text are given a green knife and
fork symbol). Each region also gets its own colour,
and this is used down the edge of the page and
throughout that regional section.

Send us your feedback We love to hear from
readers – your comments help make our books better. We read every word you send us, and we always
guarantee that your feedback goes straight to the
appropriate authors. The most useful submissions are
rewarded with a free book. To send us your updates
and find out about Lonely Planet events, newsletters
and travel news visit our award-winning website:
lonelyplanet.com/contact.

Note: We may edit, reproduce and incorporate
your comments in Lonely Planet products such as
guidebooks, websites and digital products, so let us
know if you don't want your comments reproduced or
your name acknowledged. For a copy of our privacy
policy visit **lonelyplanet.com/privacy**.

Mixed Sources
Product group from well-managed
forests and other controlled sources
www.fsc.org Cert no. SGS-COC-005002
© 1996 Forest Stewardship Council
FSC

RYAN VER BERKMOES

Ryan Ver Berkmoes first visited Bali in 1993. On his visits since he has explored almost every corner of the island. Just when he thinks he's sampled every beach on the island, he goes down a little track and finds another sandy cove. Better yet, he simply never tires of the place. Five visits in two years shows this – sometimes his Bali social calendar is busier than anywhere else. Off-island, Ryan lives in Portland, Oregon and vows to sample every last microbrew in town – a lifetime avocation.

RYAN'S THANKS

This list just seems to grow. Many thanks to friends like Hanafi, Jeremy Allan, Eliot Cohen, Jamie James, Mary Justice Thomasson-Croll, Kerry and Milton Turner, Adyus, Kadek Gunarta, Ibu Cat, Patricia Miklautsch, Rucina Ballinger, Jack Daniels, Marilyn, Wayan Suarnata, Chrystine Hanley and many more. Seeing my friends in Bali always makes me want to double my stay while tripling the fun.

Our readers Many thanks to the travellers who wrote to us with helpful hints, useful advice and interesting anecdotes: Torsten Elsner, Simon Jones

Cover photograph Melasti ceremony on Kuta Beach celebrating Balinese New Year, Andrew Brownbill/Lonely Planet Images. **Internal photographs** p44, p50, p76, p97, p112 by Ryan Ver Berkmoes. All other photographs by Lonely Planet Images; p10, p12, p23, p25, p26, p124, p129 Gregory Adams; p6, p20, p42, p95 Jerry Alexander; p21 Michael Aw; p127 John Banagan; p19, p27, p99 Paul Beinson; p105 Anders Blomquist; p58 John Borthwick; p4, p28, p38, p74 Andrew Brownbill; p86 Tom Cockrem; p28 Andrew Cubran; p28 Greg Elms; p14, p30 Alain Evrard; p121 Michael Gebicki; p68, p80, p102 Richard I'Anson; p6 Dennis Jones; p32, p60, p70, p126 Paul Kennedy; p110 Margie Politzes; p106 Tim Rock; p17, p48, p114 Wibowo Rusli; p6 Douglas Steakly; p22 Lawrence Worcester; p16, p18, p40, p53, p54, p65, p77, p91, p116, p120, p122, p123, p125 Stephanie Victor.

All images are copyright of the photographers unless otherwise indicated. Many of the images in this guide are available for licensing from **Lonely Planet Images:** www.lonelyplanetimages.com.

Cultural relics and natural beauty – Bali at its best

THIS IS BALI

Bali packs a lot into a little island. A single day can bring more sights, adventures and discoveries than a week's worth of travel elsewhere.

A religious procession brings the tourist-thronged streets of Seminyak to a stop, a dancer displays trance-like artistry at an Ubud cultural pavilion, a diver is transfixed by an untouched reef, a surfer finds the perfect break, a walker rubs her eyes trying to cope with the lush green beauty of the surrounding rice paddies, a jaded tourist is charmed by an unexpected act of kindness by a local – all of these things are part of a typical day in Bali. This is a destination that rises far above a typical tropical island destination by virtue of its culture, scenery and people.

Where else will you find intricate little offerings to the gods placed in serene little niches at world-class resorts? Or see a dance show with movements and music performed by a village dance troupe that has been perfecting their act for generations? And amid myriad palms and other lush growth, where else can you find sinuous ribbons of rice growing on green terraces wrapping around the hills?

Yes, Bali has many splendid beaches but it has so much more, from the world-class restaurants and nightlife of south Bali to hidden villages where travellers can escape the tourist hubbub and much of modern life as well. And it's all wrapped up in a rich and intriguing culture you'll find nowhere else.

It's also affordable in Bali. World-class meals and lodgings and an exhausting nightlife can be enjoyed by everyone; stay an extra day! It's no matter if you're on a surfer budget or willing to leave the bills to the little people, a day of delights in Bali won't have you singing the blues when you go home. Rather, you might just find yourself humming a gamelan tune, remembering your days in paradise.

Top left Rich greens of the rice terraces of Tabanan **Top right** A man considers many things, looking out over the rocks
Bottom The much-photographed temple complex of Pura Tanah Lot (p114)

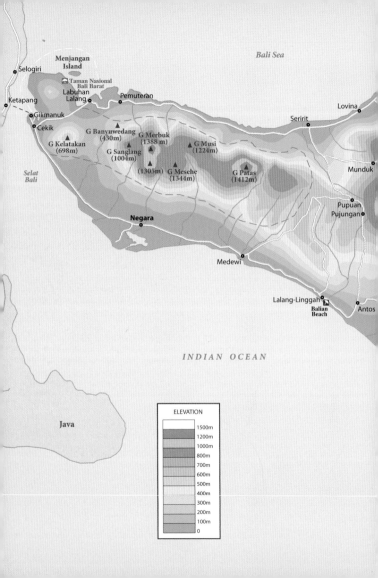

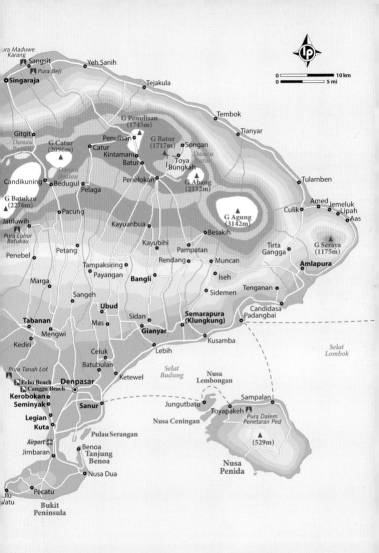

>HIGHLIGHTS

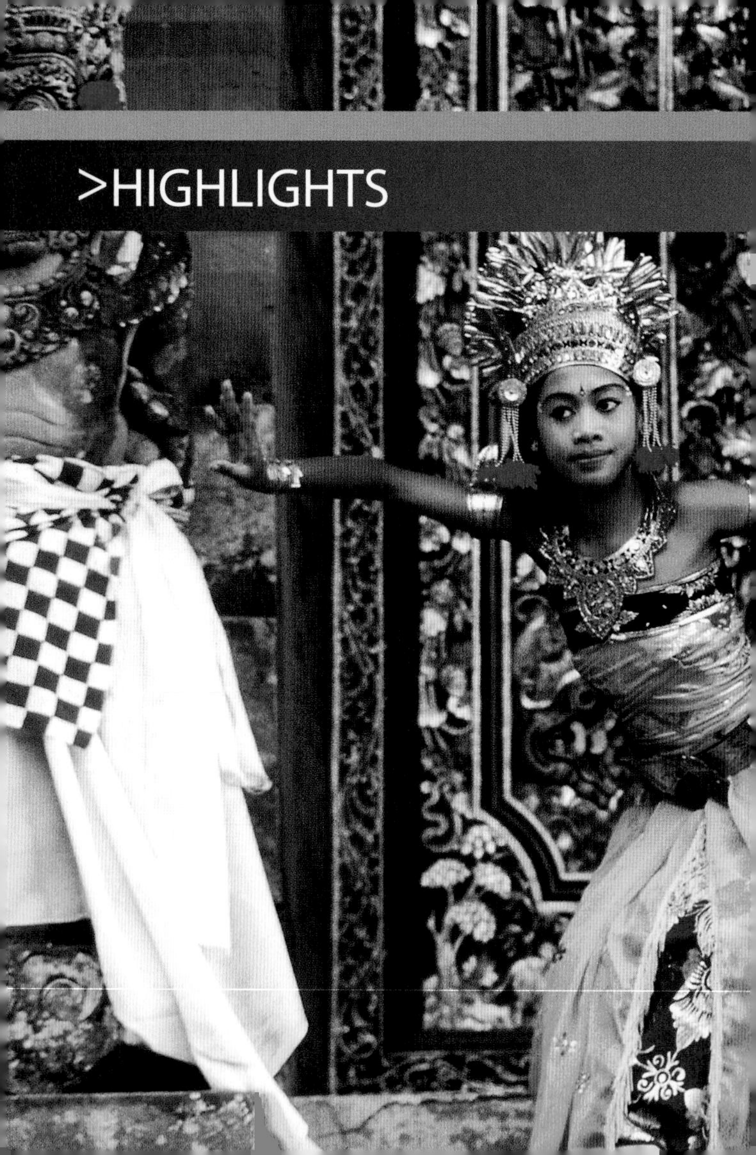

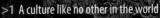
The dancing is exquisite, as always

>1 BALI'S CULTURE

A CULTURE LIKE NO OTHER IN THE WORLD

Name another tropical resort where a busy street will suddenly close and a parade of extravagantly dressed people will go zipping by. Many will be carrying huge pyramids of showroom-quality fruit or elaborate woven baskets filled with offerings. Maybe two men will march past hoisting an entire roast pig. And then, as quickly as it started, the crowd is past and traffic resumes, leaving a few slack-jawed tourists pondering the images on their cameras.

OK, many places have parades for special occasions or holidays, but in Bali a procession can happen at any time. And happen they do, daily. The Balinese are deeply spiritual and much of their daily life is devoted to religious matters. But these aren't the 'You're damned and going to hell' spoilsports of some faiths; rather, Bali's version of Hinduism is an all-pervasive effort to bring out the best in the gods and spirits. Turn a corner in even the crappiest part of Kuta and there will be an exquisite little offering sitting serenely, a ribbon of smoke still trailing up from the incense. Meaning is everywhere. Those

enormous, artful kites you see overhead in South Bali? They are a way to get the ear of the gods to suggest that a bountiful harvest would be a very nice thing. That little shrine with a carved statue wearing a black-and-white checked sarong (it symbolises good and evil) that otherwise seems forgotten? Well, it's not. On its appointed day the streets will suddenly close and a merry mob will appear to show respect.

Although modern life continues to transform life in Bali, the devotion of the people is impressive. As expat business owners often grouse, they have to hire twice as many people as they need because half the staff are always off for a ceremony. But skip your obligations to earn more money? It's not even a consideration. Young girls still take Balinese dance lessons and boys learn to play the gamelan, and even if most of the paying audiences are tourists, look behind the curtains at a performance in Ubud and you'll see a small crowd enjoying the show. Walk down a street and you'll hear ceremonial bands wildly practising. Turn up on Nyepi (see p24) and you'll see the entire island turn off.

>2 BEACHES
POUND THE SAND, SWIM THE SEA

Bali is ringed with beaches, which is one of the reasons all those planes keep landing at the airport. None are as stunning as those you'll find in places like the Caribbean or even the coast of New South Wales, but they come in so many forms that there's virtually a beach for everyone. There's a reason that tourism started in Kuta: just look at that beach (p38). It disappears in both directions and has ceaselessly crashing waves, which at their best are long aqua ribbons twisting into white. On Sundays the beach is thronged with locals taking timid steps into the water; on any day massage women languidly ply their trade while men offer up beers from coolers at prices that will cause you to ask for two. Vacationers claim a part of the beach they like, make friends with the vendors and return to 'their' beach for the rest of their trip. Meanwhile, surfers come and go, hopping across the hot road. And up towards Seminyak (p49) pick-up football and volleyball games mix visitors with locals.

Go as far as Echo Beach (p60) and the crowds get small and the surf gets large. South of the airport, the vast arid rock that is the Bukit Peninsula harbours a score of beaches (p66) sheltering in tiny coves below the cliffs. Coming closest to the white-sand cliché, these remote idylls are good for watching the world-class surfing offshore amid beautiful surrounds.

Meanwhile, in Tanjung Benoa and Sanur families frolic on mellow beaches picked clean daily. Walkways follow the strands allowing for relaxed strolling from one resort to the next. Things get wild again going east. Eastern beaches (p103) are often empty. Waves pound the dark volcanic sand, which is flecked with mica that produces a magical sparkle in the sun. In Padangbai (p102), a little lunette of sand near the ferry terminal is backed by simple guesthouses that embody the sort of funky vibe that has fuelled generations of backpacker travels. Finally, catch a boat across the surprisingly lively channel to Nusa Lembongan (p106), where a long strip of sand brings together surfers, divers, locals and travellers in a scene that's among the best in Bali.

HIGHLIGHTS

>3 SHOPPING STREETS

DISCOVERING RETAIL PLEASURES

Fortify yourself with a coffee or juice, then start your walk east along Jl Oberoi and prepare for the delights ahead. This street, one of Bali's best shopping strips (broken pavement and all), never ceases to delight. For one there's always a new surprise; yesterday's hot designer has seemingly evaporated, replaced by a new sensation. Eavesdrop on a table of designers at the Corner Store (p52) and you might get the scoop. Continue around on Jl Raya Seminyak and there's a lot more than just fashion. Oddball beads, museum-quality baskets and a glam purse worthy of Rihanna are among the finds. At Jl Double Six hang a right and head to the beach, passing a panoply of fab fabric wholesalers and bikini-makers. Just another shopping trip in Bali.

>4 RICE FIELDS

FINDING FERTILE FIELDS OF MAGIC

Beaches? Yeah, they're fun but the most arresting scenery in Bali is the rice fields. From the rolling paddies in and around Ubud (p88) to the jaw-dropping vistas of Jatiluwih (p115) to the amphitheatres of green near Sidemen (p102), there's a magic that pervades the fields. Maybe it's because they are so alive. And we don't just mean the fast-growing slender stalks. It starts at the ground where water continually courses from one field to the next (called *subak*, the system is classically Balinese in that it ensures that everybody gets their share, even if you're the last farmer downhill). People in conical hats walk the dividing ridges, sometimes followed by ducks cheerfully quacking their way to another field for a feast (it's another fine Balinese solution: rice-eating snails and bugs go in one end, fertiliser comes out the other). Scarecrows wave off birds, while flags signal the gods to be generous. Magic.

>5 WALKING

GO TAKE A HIKE

It's easy to miss the little things in Bali – and we don't mean that tiny temple offering you just squashed (don't worry, it's expected they'll get squashed). We mean all the little details that set it apart from other places. Simple shrines, an obscured bit of art, a fanciful carving or an exquisite little orchid are best appreciated if you slow down enough to first take notice. The best way to do this? Take a walk. Much of Bali is perfect for walking (we're ignoring the many challenges of urban pavements here). It can be as simple as hitting the sand in Seminyak (p49) and Kuta (p38) and heading out past scores of happy people basking in the sun. Or you can explore the backstreets of Ubud or penetrate the misty tropical forests of Munduk (p111). No matter where you walk in Bali, you're sure to discover your own details.

>6 SURFING

YOU'LL NEVER BE BORED WITH A BOARD

Listen to the accents of the surfers: Australian, American, Italian, Dutch, Japanese, Balinese (yes, lots of Balinese!) and many more are heard. People from all over the world come to Bali to surf, which shouldn't surprise anyone. Bali's surf breaks are legend and they are many. The series off Ulu Watu (p70) are among the world's best. Just look at the morning traffic jams of board-carrying motorbikes heading south from Kuta. And it's not just the rad waves far to the south. Gnarly surf can be found across Bali: in the west (p115), out on Nusa Lembongan (p106) and close in from Seminyak (p49) to Kuta (p38). In fact there's no need to be a poser. Bali's main visitor beach is lined with surf schools and when it comes time to don the look, there's entire retail empires owned by people who were once just surfers, dude (p40).

HIGHLIGHTS

>7 SYBARITE'S BALI
RELISH, REVEL, RELAX

Grab the penis and knock it on the little man's head. Soon a big man appears, ready to supply you with anything you need. It's a perfect moment at one of our favourite hotels in Bali and encapsulates why this is really an island of indulgence. The little knocker is a typically Balinese bit of whimsy: a carved wooden statue used to call for service. The staffer is the opposite of stiff: he might just plop down on a chair for a chat while you decide if you want a perfectly chilled G&T, a plate of warm nuts or maybe you'll just go straight to the Bollinger. Lavish five-star hotels aren't unusual at popular resort destinations, but in Bali they come with an intangible extra spirit and sense of fun taken right from the island itself.

>8 UNDERWATER BALI

MAKING FRIENDS UNDERWATER

The sunfish stared at me and I stared back. And while rude, I couldn't help it as he didn't look like any fish I'd seen before. Maybe 3m long but much taller, he was a stoic apparition drifting past in the current. 'Wow' was all I could think. My brief acquaintance with the sunfish (or *mola-mola*) was not unique. These huge creatures are found at many spots around Bali, as are a huge variety of other fish and mammals, from parrot fish to whales. The coral reefs and cliffs of Menjangan Island (p113) offer some of the finest diving and snorkelling in Southeast Asia. Other worthy places to take the plunge include Tulamben (p108), where you can shore dive (or snorkel) out to a wrecked WWII freighter, and Nusa Lembongan (p106), which has sites ranging from mangroves to reefs to cliffs off nearby Nusa Penida. In Bali, you may not want to come up for air.

>9 PEOPLE
LET THE LOCALS CHAT YOU UP

'Where do you come from?' and 'Where do you stay?' are two questions you'll hear throughout your stay in Bali (besides 'Transport?'). It's easy to brush them off as needlessly invasive, the prelude to a scam or just clutter in your time spent relaxing. But to do so would be rude and rudeness is one of the high crimes of Balinese society (yes, drivers honk their horns all the time, but it's to say 'Here I am' rather than 'Get out of my way' – and did you ever notice how everybody gets to merge?). Rather, these two basic questions stem from centuries of culture when people were identified by their village. And where you're staying helps identify who you are. So have a chat, it's your entrée into Bali society.

>BALI DIARY

At times Bali seems like one long celebration. Religious festivals abound and temple ceremonies and processions seem to rocket out of nowhere. For visitors the great thing is that for most events in Balinese life, including the stunning cremation ceremonies, outsiders are welcome. However, the difficult aspect is that few events in Bali follow any kind of schedule. Many are governed by the *saka* and *wuku* calendars (see www.balinesia.com/calendar/index.html) that have 210 days in a year, while other events such as temple ceremonies occur on days deemed especially propitious. So something special will happen while you're in Bali – it's just likely to be a surprise.

Stunning silks and jewels are worn for the weaving dance at the Bali Arts Festival (p24)

WUKU FESTIVALS

The *wuku* calendar is used to determine festival dates. The calendar uses 10 different types of weeks between one and 10 days long, which all run simultaneously. The intersection of the various weeks determines auspicious days. A full year is made up of 30 individually named seven-day weeks (210 days).

Galungan, which celebrates the death of a legendary tyrant called Mayadenawa, is one of Bali's major festivals. During this 10-day period, all the gods come down to earth for the festivities. Barong (mythical lion-dog creatures) prance from temple to temple and village to village, and locals rejoice with feasts and visits to families. The celebrations culminate with the Kuningan festival, when the Balinese say thanks and goodbye to the gods.

Every village in Bali will celebrate Galungan and Kuningan in grand style. If you're in Bali during these times, you'll have a ball.

MARCH & APRIL

Nyepi (the Day of Silence)

Bali's major Hindu festival, Nyepi celebrates the end of the old year and the start of the new one. It's marked by a complete lack of activity to convince evil spirits that Bali is uninhabited, so they will leave the island alone for another year (also see boxed text, below).

CHILLING BALI STYLE

Following the *saka* calendar, Nyepi falls somewhere between mid-March and early April, and usually coincides with the end of the rainy season. The Day of Silence lasts for 24 hours from sunrise, and during this time all shops, bars and restaurants close. No one is allowed to leave their home and foreigners must stay in their hotels (which provide simple meals); even Bali's airport is closed. Upcoming dates: 4 April 2011, 23 March 2012, 12 March 2013.

Bali Spirit Festival

Ubud gets excited – albeit in a very calm way – for this multiday celebration (www. balispiritfestival.com) of yoga, dance and music. Headquartered at the Yoga Barn (p92), the festival attracts scores to venues across town, especially to the big-name concerts.

MID-JUNE TO MID-JULY

Bali Arts Festival

Denpasar's annual arts festival (www .baliartsfestival.com) is the premier event on Bali's cultural calendar. Based at the Taman Wedhi Budaya arts centre (Map p85, E1), the festival is a splendid way to see traditional Balinese dance and music. Scores of village-based dance and musical groups compete fiercely for local pride.

BALI DIARY

Looking beautiful, a dancer from Bungaya waits for the opening of the Bali Arts Festival (p24)

JULY

Bali Kite Festival

Travel in South Bali and you'll see scores of kites overhead much of the year.

Often huge (10m or more in length), they can fly at altitudes that worry pilots. There's a spiritual connection: the kites are there to urge the gods to provide abundant harvests.

A GOOD DAY FOR...

Look inside a Balinese home or business and you're likely to see a copy of the *Kalendar Cetakan* hanging on a wall. This annual publication tracks the various local religious calendars and overlays them upon the 365-day Western calendar. The calendar lists which days are best for myriad activities, such as bull castration, building a boat, laying a foundation, drilling a well, starting a long trip and having sex. Many Balinese would not think of scheduling any activity without checking the calendar first: a potential spanner in the works since some activities are only condoned for a few days a year (except sex, which is called for at least 10 days a month – a real marketing tool!).

FINDING A FESTIVAL

To outsiders, religious and other ceremonial events seem to happen at random – and that's one of Bali's real charms. Sitting in a cafe only to see the street suddenly closed off and a procession come streaming past is a purely Balinese experience. Temple ceremonies are huge celebrations that bring out locals in their silks and other fineries. Offerings are often lavish and artful. So how to find one while you're on the island? Ask a local. The Balinese are highly attuned to ceremonies and can always tell you what is happening. Many of the elaborate decorations take days or even weeks to prepare so plans begin far in advance and anticipation builds.

Flower decorations at the Bali Arts Festival (p24)

OCTOBER

Kuta Karnival

A big beach party on the big beach in Kuta (www.kutakarnival.com); games, art, competitions, surfing and much more on the first October weekend and the days right before.

Ubud Writers & Readers Festival

This Ubud festival (www.ubudwritersfestival.com) brings together scores of writers and readers from around the world in a celebration of writing – especially that which touches on Bali. Its reputation is growing by the year.

Ready to party at Double Six Club (p45) in Legian

ITINERARIES

Small in size but big on opportunity, Bali can be daunting: so much to see and do, so little time. The key is managing your expectations. Don't overplan, make a few decisions and enjoy – you can always come back. If time's on your side, then frolic through everything listed here.

THREE DAYS

Let the magic fingers get that jet lag out of your system at Jari Menari (p48): you've no time for sloth. In fact, you don't have time to rest, so party on! Stay and play in Seminyak. Hit the beach (p49) and shop (p49) by day, and surf the scene (p55) at night. Blur the definitions between night and day at some of the clubs like Double Six (p45) on the cusp of Seminyak.

ONE WEEK

Now you've got time to relax. You can have a cultural immersion in Ubud (p88) but why not try various bits of Bali? Sanur (p78) is perfectly located to enjoy the best of Bali. Everything from rice terraces in the east (p100) and hidden beaches at Ulu Watu (p70) to the nightlife of Kuta (p45) is an hour or less away. A day trip snorkelling Nusa Lembongan's reefs (p106) is easy-peasy. Pop into Denpasar (p84) too.

TWO WEEKS

Split your time. Spend a week in a beachy redoubt between Kerobokan (p56) and Jimbaran (p62). Then it's off to Ubud (p88): slow down and get into the rhythm of Balinese culture. Go for walks (p93), take day trips into the mountains (p110) and at night see some dance (p98). Debate you favourite troupe over a meal at Three Monkeys (p98). Plunge into a temple celebration or a cremation ceremony; let the tourist office (p98) show you where.

LIVE LIKE A LOCAL

Skip bland tourist food and just say 'no' to a Bintang T-shirt. Experience Bali like a local: hit the huge markets in Denpasar (p86) followed by

Top left Like to live dangerously? Hang about on high, Sanur **Top right** Just going places on another lovely day, Denpasar **Bottom** Sunset over Gunung Agung (p110), Bali's highest and most revered mountain

V

ITINERARIES

lunch (p87) at a place where you might just exclaim the equivalent of 'I can see!' (ie 'I can taste!'). Blissfully fed, you'll understand why any time can be nap time in Bali. Head up to Pura Luhur Batukau (p115) where you can commune with the gods and take a nap alongside a babbling brook.

GET AN EYEFUL

Sometimes you just want to enjoy the view. Start at Pura Luhur Ulu Watu (p68) for entrancing views of the steady march of swells from across the ocean. Stop at Garuda Wisnu Kencana Cultural Park (p68) for vistas across the south and beyond to the volcanos, your next stop. High in the hills at Munduk (p111) find your perfect waterfall and view the sweep of forests and orchards down to the sharp contrast where land meets the sea. Finally, boat out to Nusa Lembongan (p106), where you can nurse a coldie while you gaze upon all of Bali.

Pura Luhur Ulu Watu (p68) visitors gaze out over the Bukit Peninsula and the pounding surf

FORWARD PLANNING

Three weeks before you go Check to see that your passport is good to go and that you don't need a visa (p141). Book your accommodation (although Bali's popularity means that earlier rather than later is better). Compare lots of sites before you choose – different hotels cut deals with different websites. Check the calendar to see if your trip coincides with any major holidays. If it's Nyepi (p24) bring an extra book and maybe a candle. Start reading the newsy websites (p145) so you can see what people are talking about.

Two weeks before you go Book a massage at Jari Menari (p48) for when you arrive. Let the dancing fingers walk away with your jet lag. Learn your vital 50 words of Indonesian: please (*silahkan*), thank you (*terima kasih*) et al. If you are taking new shoes, start wearing them so breaking them in doesn't break you down.

The day before you go Make certain your address book is online so you can email beach photos to the suckers back home. Measure yourself in case you see something adorable. Make a currency exchange cheat sheet (www.xe.com) so you can see if you can afford it. Buy a trashy beach novel (but not *Eat, Pray, Love* – don't be a cliché!).

FREELY ACTIVE

If you have your own board you can surf all you want for free. But you don't even need a board to get active in Bali. You don't even need cash: hit the beach in Seminyak at Double Six (p49) and join a pick-up game of football or volleyball. In Sanur follow a kite string (p25) to the owners and offer to help keep the huge beast from pulling everybody to Lombok – they'll love you for it. In Ubud you can walk and hike (p93) until you need new shoes. You might need to spring for shades – there's all that dazzling green.

>REGIONS

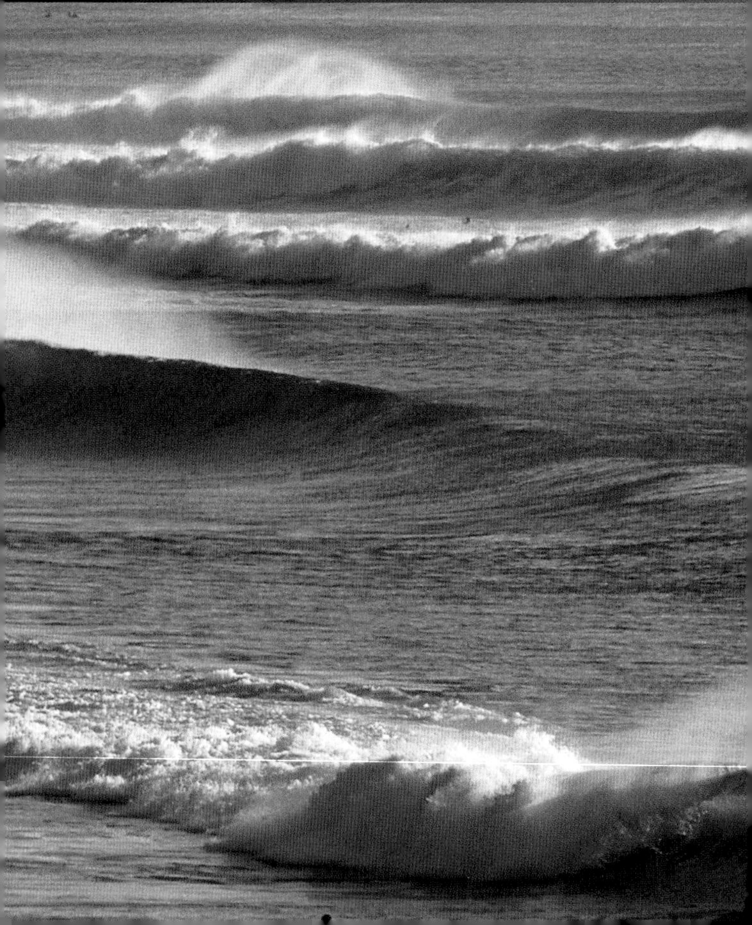

These waves on the Bukit Peninsula (p66) call to surfers from all over the world

>REGIONS

Who knew you could fit so much into such a small place? Bali has an amazing diversity of regions crowded across the island, like so many offerings at a temple festival.

Bali is insanely convenient for visitors. Tired of one area? Something completely different is close by, often just a short walk away on the beach. Kuta is the original tourist hub. Its very name causes some to shudder with delight and others to shudder with horror. Yet a quick stroll along the iconic beach and you're in Seminyak, which couldn't be any more different thanks to its posh hotels and dozens of designer shops. Its greatest similarities to Kuta are two: it has that beach and people either love or hate it.

South of the airport, the Bukit Peninsula is the barren alternative to that Balinese vision of endless green rice fields. Again, there's a sharp divide in just one little peninsula. On the west are the legendary surf breaks around Ulu Watu. Funky guesthouses cling to the cliffs while surfers enjoy epic rides below. Go east to Nusa Dua and Tanjung Benoa and you find tiny waves lapping at reef-protected beaches, fronted by a string of huge hotels, while package tourists zip past in banana boats.

Across the channel and up the coast, Sanur serenely steers the middle ground, offering a little bit of everything. The bustling capital Denpasar offers entry into the best food and shopping experiences. Move up the hillside and you discover the heart of Balinese culture in Ubud. The magical notes of gamelans echo through the quiet streets at night, while those seeking something special browse around art galleries by day.

Head east and you can almost lose yourself in sinuous roads wandering through lush valleys, palm-topped hills and an often wild and untamed coast.

Within a drive of an hour or two you can enjoy several Balis. Choose your favourites, but enjoy several.

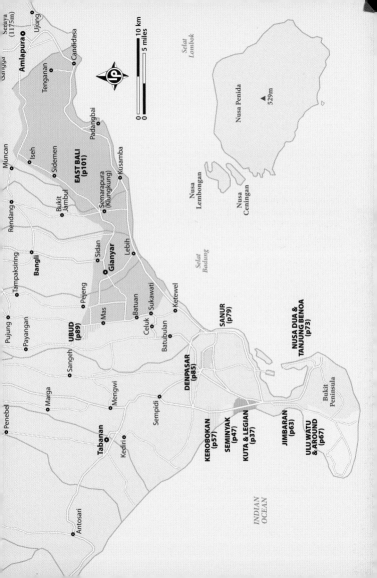

>KUTA & LEGIAN

Teeming, mad, crazy, nutty, wild, loud. Those are a few words that describe Kuta and Legian, the original tourist centre of Bali and the place that everyone either loves to hate or loves to love. Kuta's the original, with its narrow alleys (gangs), hawkers, tawdry bars, cheap hotels and open-air cafes peddling cheap Bintang and nonthreatening nasi goreng (fried rice). Every third person you see is carrying a surfboard, every fourth sports a fresh tattoo. If you're in Bali to party, live cheap and stumble to the beach, this is the place for you. Legian, Kuta's sister just to the north, is marginally quieter. It's the place Kuta-lovers go after they've had kids. The streets, hotels and bums are all wider, but it's still a place where partying comes first and cultural pursuits a distant second.

KUTA & LEGIAN

🏃 DO

AJ Hackett Bungy	1	A1
Jamu Spa	2	B4
Naruki Surf Shop	3	C4
Putri Bali	4	B2
Rip Curl School of Surf	5	A1
Waterbom Park	6	B6

🛍 SHOP

Rip Curl	7	B6
Surfer Girl	8	C5

🍴 EAT

Balcony	9	B4
Indo-National	10	B3
Kori Restaurant & Bar	11	C5
Made's Warung	12	C6
Mama's	13	C4
Poppies Restaurant	14	C5
Take	15	C3
Warung Asia	16	A1
Warung Indonesia	17	C5
Warung Murah	18	A1
Warung Yogya	19	B3
Zanzibar	20	A1

🍸 DRINK

De Ja Vu	21	A1
Legend	22	B3
Sky Garden Lounge	23	C5

⭐ PLAY

Apache Reggae Bar	24	C5
Bounty	25	C5
DeeJay Cafe	26	B6
Double Six Club	27	A1
Mbargo	28	C5

Double Six
Beach

Gate

See Seminyak
Map p47

Jl Double Six (Jl Arjuna)

Jl Pura Bagus Taruna
(Jl Werkudara)

Jl Padma Utara

Gate
Gate

Legian
Beach

Gate

Jl Padma (Jl Yudistra)

Jl Sahadewa

Jl Sadewa

Legian

Jl Melasti

Jl Majapahit

Teluk
Kuta

Jl Pantai Kuta (Kuta Beach Rd)

Jl Benesari

Jl Pura Puseh

Sungai Mati

Jl Patih Jelantik

Jl Imam Bonjol

Poppies Gang II
(Jl Batu Bolong)

Kuta
Beach

Kuta

Gang Sorga

Gang Bedugul

Jl Pantai Banjar Pande Mas

Sorga
Gang

Poppies Gang I

Bemo
Corner

Jl Pantai Kuta

Jl Tengal Wangi

Jl Kartika Plaza
(Jl Dewi Sartika)

Kuta sq

Jl Bakung Sari (Jl Singasari)

Jl Buni
Sari

Jl Raya Kuta

Jl Blambangan

Jl Ngurah Rai Bypass

Jl Sunset

0 ——— 400 m
0 ——— 0.2 miles

SEE

KUTA BEACH

This long ribbon of golden sand and picture-perfect surf is the reason tourism started here in the first place. Always crowded with locals and tourists alike, you can get a cheap massage, drink a cold beer, gaze out to sea or ride a wave. And that's just in the morning.

DO

AJ HACKETT BUNGY

☎ 0361-731144; Jl Arjuna; US$99; ☻ noon-8pm daily & 2-6am Fri & Sat

Beside the beach at the Double Six Club in Legian, it has a great view of the coast (it means you can't see the hideous tower you're standing on – or bouncing from). Try not to load up on much of anything before you take the plunge.

JAMU SPA

☎ 0361-752520; www.jamutraditional spa.com; Alam Kul Kul, Jl Pantai Kuta; traditional massage US$45; ☻ 9am-9pm

In serene surrounds at a resort hotel, you can enjoy indoor massage rooms that open onto a pretty garden courtyard. If you've ever wanted to be part of a fruit cocktail, here's your chance – treatments involve tropical nuts, coconuts, papayas and more, often in fragrant baths.

Getting around Kuta style

☒ NARUKI SURF SHOP
☎ 0361-765772; off Poppies Gang II; 🕙 10am-7pm
One of dozens of surf shops lining the *gangs* of Kuta, the friendly guys here will rent you a board, fix your ding, offer advice or give you lessons.

☒ PUTRI BALI
☎ 0361-755987; Wisata Beach Inn, Jl Padma Utara; massage from 75,000Rp; 🕙 10am-9pm
Locals swear by the cream bath; it has sent many a spa-o-phile's heart a-flutter with delight. Located just off the main street, this lovely spa is excellent value. A two-hour program of healthful pleasures costs a mere 175,000Rp.

☒ RIP CURL SCHOOL OF SURF
☎ 0361-735858; www.ripcurlschoolof surf.com; Jl Arjana; lessons from US$59
Usually universities sell shirts with their logos; here it's the other way round: the beachwear company sponsors a school. You can learn to surf at the popular Double Six beach.

☒ WATERBOM PARK
☎ 0361-755676; www.waterbom.com; Jl Kartika Plaza; adult/child US$23/13; 🕙 9am-6pm; 👶
Just south of Kuta, this watery amusement park covers 3.5 hectares of landscaped tropical

PICK A NAME, ANY NAME
A small lane or alley is known as a *gang*, and most of them in Bali lack signs or even names. Some are referred to by the name of a connecting street, eg Jl Padma Utara is the *gang* going north of Jl Padma. Many are too small for cars, although this doesn't seem to stop some drivers from causing chaos. (When this happens, grab a beer in a cafe and watch.)

Many streets in Kuta and Legian have more than one name. *Gangs* and roads that took the names of early tourist destinations (like Poppies) are being given new more culturally aware names. But this being Bali, everyone uses *all* the names. In this guide all the various names are shown on the maps, but in the text, the street name that the business uses is the one given. Here are the various names in use in Kuta and Legian.

Old/unofficial	New/official
Jl Double Six	Jl Arjuna
Jl Pura Bagus Taruna/ Rum Jungle Rd	Jl Werkudara
Jl Padma	Jl Yudistra
Poppies Gang II	Jl Batu Bolong
Jl Pantai Kuta	Jl Pantai Banjar Pande Mas
Jl Kartika Plaza	Jl Dewi Sartika

gardens. It has assorted water slides, swimming pools, play areas, a supervised park for children

REGIONS

KUTA & LEGIAN

under five years old, and a 'lazy river' ride. Other indulgences include the 'pleasure pool', a food court and bar, and a spa.

SHOP

RIP CURL *Surfer*
☎ 0361-765035; Kuta Sq
Cast that mopey black stuff aside and make a bit of a splash! This mothership of the surfwear giant has a huge range of beach clothes, water wear and surfboards.

SURFER GIRL *Surfer*
☎ 0361-752693; Jl Legian 138
A local legend, the winsome logo says it all about this vast store

for girls of all ages. Clothes, gear, bikinis and plenty of other stuff in every shade of bubblegum ever made.

It's a cool, cool look inside the Surfer Girl shop (above)

🍴 EAT

🍴 BALCONY *Western* $$
☎ 0361-757409; Jl Benesari 16

The Balcony has a breezy tropical design and sits above the hub-bub below. It's a good place to celebrate an excellent day spent riding the waves; you can wash down grilled steaks and seafood with various fruity drinks. This is a great spot for breakfast.

🍴 INDO-NATIONAL
Western, Seafood $$
☎ 0361-759883; Jl Padma 17; ♿

Kerry and Milton Turner's popular restaurant is home away from home for legions of happy fans. Grab a cold one with the rest of the crew up the front at the bar while you take in the sweeping view of Legian's action. Or head back to a pair of shady and roman-tic tables. Order the heaped-up grilled seafood platter and Bali's best garlic bread; the prawn toast is also tops.

🍴 KORI RESTAURANT & BAR
Western, Steaks $$
☎ 0361-758605; Poppies Gang II

Kori's tables weave through a se-ries of gardens and ponds. It has a good selection of pasta, upmarket Indonesian, burgers and more. It's ideal for a secluded rendezvous over a nonclichéd tropical drink in the flower-bedecked nooks out

the back (or have one of the fabled gin and tonics). Some nights there's live acoustic music.

🍴 MADE'S WARUNG
Indonesian $$
☎ 0361-755297; Jl Pantai Kuta

Made's was the original tourist warung (food stall) in Kuta. Through the years, the Western-ised Indonesian menu has been much copied. Classic dishes such as *nasi campur* (rice served with side dishes) are served with colour and flair.

🍴 MAMA'S *German* $$
☎ 0361-761151; Jl Legian; ⏱ 24hr

This German classic serves schnit-zel and other meaty dishes around the clock. The beer (good local Storm plus a few kegs of brews that have made the long voyage from the homeland) comes by the litre and the open-air bar is a merry place for enjoying satellite sports. This is the best place in South Bali for a European-style breakfast.

🍴 POPPIES RESTAURANT
Western, Indonesian $$
☎ 0361-751059; Poppies Gang I

Poppies was one of the first restaurants to be established in Kuta (Poppies Gang I is even named after it). Apart from its foody reputation, it is popular

REGIONS

KUTA & LEGIAN

Nasi goreng – and what could that possibly be on the side?

for its lush garden setting. There are little pebbles underfoot and it feels slightly mysterious in a romantic way. The delicious food is upmarket Western and Balinese. It's just across from the gracious cottages of the same name.

🍴 TAKE *Japanese, Sushi* $$
☎ 0361-759745; Jl Patih Jelantik
Flee Bali for Tokyo just by ducking under the traditional fabric shield over the door. Hyper-fresh sushi, sashimi and more are prepared under the fanatical eyes of a team of chefs behind a long counter. Dine at low tables or hang out in a booth.

🍴 WARUNG ASIA
Asian, Cafe $
☎ 0361-742 0202; off Jl Double Six & Jl Pura Bagus Taruna
Look down a couple of little *gang* for this gem: traditional Thai dishes served in a stylish open-air cafe, an authentic Italian espresso machine and lots of newspapers to peruse.

🍴 WARUNG INDONESIA
Indonesian, Western $
off Poppies Gang II; 🚸
Classic Kuta. This is one of a score of similar, totally unpretentious cheapies found along the *gangs* serving up typical traveller fare

like pizza, cheap Indo standards like satay and the ubiquitous club sandwich.

🍴 WARUNG MURAH
Indonesian $
☎ 0361-732082; Jl Arjuna; **V**
Lunch goes swimmingly at this authentic warung specialising in seafood. An array of grilled fish awaits; if you prefer fowl over fin, the *satay ayam* is succulent *and* a bargain. It's close to Double Six beach and is a popular hang-out through the day. Go on, have the ultimate backpacker treat, the tasty banana pancakes.

🍴 WARUNG YOGYA
Indonesian $
☎ 0361-750835; Jl Padma Utara
Hidden in the heart of Legian, this simple warung is spotless and serves up hearty portions of local food for prices that would almost tempt a local. The *gado-gado* comes with a huge bowl of peanut sauce.

🍴 ZANZIBAR *Western* $$
☎ 0361-733529; Jl Double Six; 🛗
Always buzzing, this popular patio anchors a busy strip at Double Six beach. Sunset is prime time; the best views are from the new swath of tables on a 2nd-floor terrace. Dishes are tasty variations on Bali menu classics like the *nasi* family and the burger bunch.

🍸 DRINK

🍸 DE JA VU *Music Bar*
☎ 0361-732777; Jl Arjuna; 🕐 5pm-4am
DJs are on duty from opening time every night at this high-concept, glass-fronted bar right on the busy strip at Double Six beach. Patio tables overlook the sand and sunset, but this place really shines after midnight when it is a somewhat more intimate venue than the nearby mega-clubs.

🍸 LEGEND *Music Bar*
☎ 0361-755376; Jl Sahadewa; 🕐 3pm-midnight
A popular open-air spot, Legend draws nightly crowds for 'DIY Elvis', karaoke and live music, playing everything from pop to country.

🍸 SKY GARDEN LOUNGE
Cafe-Bar
☎ 0361-756362; www.escbali.com; Jl Legian 61; 🕐 24hr
This multilevel palace of flash flirts with height restrictions from its rooftop bar where all of Kuta twinkles around you. Look for top DJs, a ground-level cafe and paparazzi-wannabes. Munchers can enjoy a long menu of bar snacks and meals (salads, sandwiches, pastas etc). Most, however, roam from floor to floor posing with posers and having a blast.

Monica Kuhon
Surfer

How long surfing in Bali? Since I came to Kuta on holiday as a child over 20 years ago. **Where now?** I often just boogie board at Echo Beach (p60) but I'll go all over. The best thing about Bali is there's always good surfing somewhere no matter the weather or the time of year. **Other favourite places?** When the waves are really big I'll go west to Balian Beach and Medewi. **What should visitors know?** If it's a month with an 'R', go east, during the other months, go west. **And?** Be polite! The local guys are really cool. I'm often the only girl out there and they stick up for me when some tourist tries to steal my wave. When there's 50 surfers at a popular spot going for the same wave, let the locals have it and try someplace else. There are so many choices.

⭐ PLAY

⭐ APACHE REGGAE BAR *Club*
☎ 0361-761212; Jl Legian 146;
🕐 11pm-4am

One of the rowdier spots in Kuta, Apache jams in locals and visitors, many of whom are on the make. The music is loud, but that pounding you feel the next day is from the free-flowing *arak* (distilled palm firewater) served in huge plastic jugs. Stumbling between here and Bounty is a Kuta tradition.

⭐ BOUNTY *Club*
☎ 0361-752529; Jl Legian;
🕐 10pm-6am

Set on a faux sailing boat amid a mini-mall of food and drink, the Bounty is a vast open-air disco that humps, thumps and pumps all night. Climb the blue-lit staircase and get down on the poop deck to hip-hop, techno, house and anything else the DJs come up with. Frequent foam parties.

⭐ DEEJAY CAFE *Club*
☎ 0361-758880; 2nd fl, Kuta Centre, off Jl Kartika Plaza 8X; 🕐 9pm-7am

The post-midnight hours see this place rocking in the post-apocalyptic Kuta Centre, the rundown remains of a mall. House DJs play tribal underground, progressive trance and more. Beware of fakers who set their alarms for 5am and arrive fresh.

⭐ DOUBLE SIX CLUB *Club*
☎ 0812-462 7733; Jl Double Six;
🕐 11pm-6am

This legendary club draws partiers from across Southeast Asia. Top international DJs play a mix of dance tunes in a sleek open-air pavilion right out of *Wallpaper** magazine. See how many drinks you can down before you decide you *have* to jump in the pool.

⭐ MBARGO *Club*
☎ 0361-756280; Jl Legian; cover from 10,000Rp; 🕐 7pm-4am

Throbs with the Gangsta vibe, enjoyed by well-heeled, sunburnt suburbanites. Hard-edged DJs encourage the sweaty throngs to misbehave. It's always ladies' night here.

>SEMINYAK

Seminyak is the upmarket counterpart up the beach from Kuta and Legian. If the priorities in the latter revolve around finding cold beer, the priorities in Seminyak involve talking about designers – or claiming to be one. Bali's poshest and most creative shops can be found here, starting on Jl Raya Seminyak and spreading out from the curving spine of Jl Oberoi and Jl Raya Petitenget. This also is where you'll find scores of restaurants from the swank trad Italian to attitudey outdoor lounges-cum–supper clubs. Top-end hotels and villas abound with the opening of a W hotel in 2009 causing much excitement. Some people's visits revolve entirely around Seminyak; others wrinkle their noses at the self-proclaimed rarefied air.

SEMINYAK

See Kerobokan Map p37

See Kuta & Legian Map p37

600 m
0.4 miles

Jl Sunset

Jl Raya Menanadi

Jl Raya Seminyak

Jl Raya Kerobokan

Jl Oberoi (Jl Laksmana)

Seminyak

Jl Dhyana Pura (Jl Abimanyu)

Jl Kayu Jati

Jl Sarinande

Jl Pantai Kaya Aya

Jl Petitenget

Jl Petitet

Teluk Kuta

👁 SEE
👁 BIASA ART SPACE
☎ 0361-847 5766 ; Jl Raya Seminyak 34;
🕙 10am-6pm

A stunning gallery owned by Susanna Perini, also owner of neighbouring Biasa shop (opposite). Changing exhibits highlight bold works by noted artists from across Southeast Asia. The space is a cool refuge from stinky, noisy Jl Legian.

👁 PURA PETITENGET
Jl Pantai Kaya Aya

This large complex, the scene of many ceremonies, is an important temple in a string of sea temples that stretches from Pura Luhur Ulu Watu on the Bukit Peninsula, north to Pura Tanah Lot in western Bali. The temple honours the visit of a 16th-century priest and is a fascinating place to ponder the intricacies of Balinese offerings.

SEMINYAK STREET NAMES
Like Kuta and Legian, Seminyak has streets with multiple names.

Old/unofficial	New/official
Jl Oberoi	Jl Laksmana
Jl Raya Seminyak	Northern stretch: Jl Raya Basangkasa
Jl Dhyana Pura/ Jl Gado Gado	Jl Abimanyu

Pura Tanah Lot (p114), one of many sea temples

🏃 DO
🏃 CHILL
☎ 0361-734701; Jl Kunti; treatments from US$13; 🕙 10am-10pm

A part of the popular and luxe Villas and Prana spa on the same street, this zen place embraces reflexology. The name says it all.

🏃 JARI MENARI
☎ 0361-736740; Jl Raya Seminyak 47; sessions from 250,000Rp; 🕙 10am-9pm

True to its name, which means 'dancing fingers', your body will be one happy dance floor. The all-male staff use massage techniques that emphasise rhythm. Many say this is the best place for a massage in Bali, a claim backed up by numerous awards.

✈ SATE BALI
☎ 0361-736734; Jl Oberoi 22; courses from 375,000Rp; ⏰ 9.30am-1pm
This excellent Balinese cooking course is taught by noted chef Nyoman Sudiyasa. Students learn to prepare Balinese spices and *sambals,* which are then used to flavour duck, fish and pork. Not up to school? The restaurant is excellent.

🛍 SHOP
🛍 BANANAS BATIK *Fabric*
☎ 0361-730938; www.bananasbatik.com; Jl Raya Seminyak
Flouncy clothes for women who equate style with comfort. The exquisite duds here are made at a little house on the ocean in East Bali. The batik is very finely made and the muted colours keep everything classy.

🛍 BIASA *Clothing*
☎ 0361-730308; www.biasabali.com; Jl Raya Seminyak 36
This is Bali-based designer Susanna Perini's premier shop. Her line of tropical wear for men and women combines cottons, silks and embroidery. The results are elegant and would pass for resortwear any place posh.

🛍 BLUE GLUE *Bikinis*
☎ 0361-844 5956; Jl Raya Seminyak
How best to show off your form on the see-and-be-seen stretches of Bali beach, especially in uber-hip Seminyak? Try one of these trendy Bali-made bathing suits.

🛍 DEZINE HAMMOCKS *Hammocks*
☎ 0361-742 2379; Jl Seminyak
Talk about a gift that keeps on giving, let alone swaying. Choose from a rainbow of hammocks in all sizes. Or have one custom-made to your exact size using the

Pascal Chevillot
Chef/owner of Sardine restaurant (p59) in Kerobokan

What's notable about food in Bali? Everything is fresh and there is huge variety. You'll find the island's top chefs in the markets buying right from the people who grow the fruits and vegetables. **What's your favourite market?** The Jimbaran fish market (p64). New seafood arrives constantly as boats pull up to the beach. You know you'll find certain things like excellent shellfish all the time but it's also an adventure as you are constantly surprised. **What's some of the best fish for sale?** Sea bream, *mahi-mahi*, skate, snapper and more. **What should visitors watch for?** They should get there as early as possible and then stay out of the way. Vendors come running with huge containers of large fish on ice. Wander around the dark interior; it's like a warren and you'll be surprised at what Bali's waters yield.

fabric of your dreams (you'll be dreaming once you hop aboard). Cost for a one-day service is about US$20.

🏠 DIVINE DIVA *Clothing*
☎ 0361-731903; Jl Oberoi 1A

It's like a Dove soap commercial for real women in this shop, filled with Bali-made breezy styles for larger figures. One customer told us: 'It's the essence of agelessness.'

🏠 ET CLUB
Clothing, Accessories
☎ 0361-730902; Jl Raya Seminyak 14A

Out-of-this-world prices on designer knock-offs and bohemian bags, belts, shoes and clothes. And should you want to set up shop at home, they'll sell by the gross.

🏠 INTI *Womenswear*
☎ 0361-733664; Jl Raya Seminyak 11

Shoppers tired of pawing through racks of size-2 clothes will sigh with relief at this shop filled with resortwear aimed at mature women.

🏠 LILY JEAN *Clothing*
☎ 0361-734864; Jl Oberoi

Saucy knickers underpin sexy women's clothing that both dares and flirts; most is Bali-made. This popular shop has flash new digs in fashion's Ground Zero.

🏠 PAUL ROPP *Clothing*
☎ 0361-734208; www.paulropp.com; Jl Oberoi

The elegant main shop for one of Bali's premier high-end fashion designers. Most goods are made just a few kilometres away in the hills above Denpasar. And what goods they are – rich silks and cottons, vivid to the point of gaudy, with hints of Ropp's roots in the tie-dyed 1960s.

🏠 PERIPLUS *Bookshop*
🕒 0361-734578; Seminyak Sq

A large outlet of the island-wide chain of lavishly fitted bookshops. Besides enough design books to have you fitting out even your garage with 'Bali Style', there's best-sellers, magazines and newspapers. In cafe-filled Seminyak Sq.

🏠 SABBATHA *Accessories*
☎ 0361-731756; Jl Raya Seminyak 97

Mega-bling! The glitter, glam and gold here are almost blinding and that's just what customers want. Opulent handbags and other sun-reflecting accessories are displayed like so much king's ransom.

🍴 EAT

🍴 BALI DELI *Deli* $$
☎ 0361-738686; Jl Kunti 117X

Almost at Jl Sunset, the lavish deli counter at this market is loaded with imported cheeses, meats and baked goods. This is the place to come for special treats for the villa or to prepare a killer picnic.

🍴 BIKU Fusion $$

☎ 0361-857 0888; Jl Petitenget

Housed in an old antique shop, Biku retains the timeless vibe of its predecessor. But there's nothing old-fashioned about the food, which combines Indonesian, other Asian and Western influences on a casual menu that's popular through the day. Dishes, from the exquisite breakfasts and the elegant local choices to Bali's best burger, are artful and delicious. There's a long list of teas and myriad refreshing cocktails. Many swoon at the sight of the cake table.

🍴 CORNER STORE Cafe $$

☎ 0361-730276; Jl Laksmana 10A; 🕒 7am-5pm

Seminyak's fashionistas gather here most mornings (aka Tuck Shop) to dish dirt and breakfast from dishes of upmarket, healthy fare like organic muesli and the always-fresh fruit. The gossip under the shady tree is hotter than the sun. High walls shelter patio diners from the perennially clogged traffic on this busy corner – as well as from prying eyes.

FOOD FOR THE MASSES

While tourists and expats chomp their way through meals at Bali's incredibly rich range of places to eat, locals flock to one of many little stalls like **Warung Ibu Made** (Jl Seminyak; 🕒 7am-7pm). The woks roar almost dawn to dusk amid the constant hubbub on this busy corner of Jl Seminyak near Jl Sunset. The simple meals from this warung couldn't be fresher and put to shame some of the Western-fakery just down the road.

🍴 EARTH CAFE
Healthfood $

☎ 0361-736645; Jl Oberoi 99; 🔲

The good vibes are organic at this vegetarian cafe and store amid the upmarket retail squalor of Seminyak. Sweet potato and garbanzo bean soup is a fine lead-in to the creative salads or wholegrain goodies. A retail section sells potions and lotions. While perusing the bookshelves, don't get ahead of yourself in the colonic irrigation section.

🍴 GROCER & GRIND
Cafe-Deli $$

☎ 081-735 4104; Jl Kayu Jati 3X

Keep your vistas limited and you might think you're just at a sleek Sydney cafe, but look around and you're unmistakeably in Bali, albeit one of the trendiest bits. Classic sandwiches, salads and big breakfasts issue forth from the kitchen. Eat in the open air or choose air-con tables in the deli area.

HU'U *Fusion* $$
☎ 0361-736443; Jl Pantai Kaya Aya;
⏱ 11am-2am

Like many of the other trendy open-air dining spots nearby, oodles of little tea candles provide a romantic glow at night. There's steak, seafood and a good selection of vegetarian dishes. Late in the evening it takes on a nightclub vibe.

LA LUCCIOLA *Fusion* $$$
☎ 0361-730838; Jl Pantai Kaya Aya

A sleek beachside restaurant with good views from the 2nd-floor tables across a lovely lawn and sand to the surf. The bar is big with sunset watchers although it's less poser-filled than some neighbours. The menu is a creative melange of international fare with an Italian flair.

TRATTORIA *Italian* $$
☎ 0361-737082; Jl Oberoi

Enjoy surprisingly authentic Italian cuisine at tables inside or out. The menu here features fresh pastas, grilled meats and seafood. The service is good and this place is justifiably popular. The wine list is a cut or two above the Bali norm.

ULTIMO *Italian* $$$
☎ 0361-738720; Jl Laksmana 104

It's simple to count your way to dining joy at this vast and always popular restaurant in the very heart of Seminyak's Eat St. *Uno:* find a table overlooking the street action, out back in one of the gardens or inside. *Due:* choose from the oh-so-very Italian menu. *Tre:* marvel at the efficient service from the army of servers. *Quattro:* smile at the reasonable bill.

Creative menu and beach views at La Lucciola

Ku De Ta attracts Bali's beautiful people to the drinks, the views and the great music

🍴 WARUNG ITALIA
Italian Warung $

☎ 0361-737437; Jl Kunti 2; ⏰ 8am-7pm; 👤

Classic Balinese warung spew forth dozens of dishes through the day. The climax happens at lunch when happy diners walk down the displays and have their plates filled with a wide selection of treats. No matter what they choose, the price is the same (and it's low). Here warung style meets Italian as diners select from a range of pastas, salads and more. Traditionalists can choose from a long menu.

🍴 ZULA VEGETARIAN PARADISE *Vegetarian* $

☎ 0361-732723; Jl Dhyana Pura 5; Ⓥ

It's all vegetarian at this ever-growing place where you can get tofu cheese, a tofu spring roll, tofu cheesecake, a tofu-chickpea burger and for the wheat-averse, brown rice.

🍸 DRINK
🍸 MANO *Cafe*

☎ 0361-730874; Petitenget Beach

Tucked away behind Pura Petitenget (p48), this basic beachside cafe overlooks a lovely and uncrowded swath of sand in otherwise busy Seminyak. Escape the crowds and fake glam elsewhere for a cold one here.

RED CARPET CHAMPAGNE BAR *Cafe-Bar*

☎ 0361-737889; Jl Oberoi 42

The closest most will come to posing for paparazzi is at this over-the-top glam bar on Seminyak's couture strip. Waltz the red carpet and toss back a few namesake flutes while contemplating a raw oyster and displays of frilly frocks. It's open to the street (but elevated dahling) so you can observe the rabble.

PLAY

KU DE TA *Club*

☎ 0361-736969; Jl Oberoi; 7am-1am

Ku De Ta teems with Bali's beautiful people (including those whose status is purely aspirational). Adults perfect their 'bored' look over drinks during the day, gazing at the fine stretch of surf right out the back. Sunset brings out crowds, who snatch a cigar at the bar or dine on eclectic fare at tables. The music throbs with increasing intensity through the night.

OBSESSION *Small Club*

☎ 0361-730269; Jl Abimanyu; 6pm-2am

Fortunately, the 'global music' at this rather intimate venue isn't more clichéd reggae. Latin, blues, soul and more get bodies grooving through the night; several neighbouring joints also cater to a mixed gay-straight crowd.

>KEROBOKAN

Kerobokan can rightly be called Seminyak North. Jl Petitenget seamlessly links the area to Seminyak. Just a few years ago this was all rice fields, but nonstop construction of boutiques, restaurants and villas has made the essential Balinese grain an endangered species. In fact, at times you may think designers – real and self-imagined – are more common. It's always worth wandering the main streets to see what's new. Although there are a few smaller hotels here, this is ground zero for private villa rentals. Featureless walled compounds line the remaining rice fields. Down by the ocean the curve of beach disappears into the mist in both directions. Many people pass through Kerobokan on their way to the trendy beaches just to the west.

KEROBOKAN

◉ SEE
Kerobokan Beach 1 A4

🏃 DO
Spa Bonita 2 C4
Umalas Stables 3 D1

🛍 SHOP
JJ Bali Button 4 E3

🍴 EAT
Café Jemme 5 D3
Fruit Market 6 E3

Sardine 7 E3
Sarong 8 C4
Waroeng Bonita ....(see 2)
Warung Batavia 9 E4
Warung Gossip 10 F2
Warung Kolega 11 C4
Warung Sulawesi 12 C3

REGIONS

KEROBOKAN

👁 SEE
👁 KEROBOKAN BEACH
Part of Bali's star beach, which stretches 15km from the airport in the south all the way north-west along the coast almost to Pura Tanah Lot (p114), the beach here has pounding surf, long and lonely stretches and a few scattered drinks vendors. Go for a serene walk!

🏃 DO
🏃 SPA BONITA
☎ 0361-731918; www.bonitabali.com; Jl Petitenget 2000X; massages from 100,000Rp; 🕙 9am-9pm
Part of the delightful Waroeng Bonita (p60), this male-oriented spa has a range of services in a simple, elegant setting.

🏃 UMALAS STABLES
☎ 0361-731402; www.balionhorse.com; Jl Lestari 9X; rides from US$72
Pick your pony in this elegant compound set among the paddies. It has a stable of 30 horses and ponies, and offers one-hour rice-field tours and two-/three-hour beach rides (a trip highlight for many tourists). Lessons in beginner to advanced equestrian events such as dressage and showjumping can also be arranged.

Horse, sand, surf, sun – perfect

🛍 SHOP
🛍 JJ BALI BUTTON *Buttons*
☎ 0361-730001; Jl Gunung Tangkuban Perahu
Zillions of beads and buttons made from shells, plastic, metal and more are displayed in what first looks like a candy store. Elaborately carved wooden buttons are 700Rp. Wander around the nearby streets, especially Jl Raya Kerobokan, for an ever-changing line-up of homeware shops, many of them more factory than showroom.

EAT

CAFÉ JEMME *Cafe* $$

☎ 0361-732392; Jl Petitenget 125;
🕐 8am-4pm; ♿

Ladies who lunch (and men too) sit primly on delicate French chairs here and gaze out at Seminyak's number-one endangered species: rice terraces. Although there's a few breakfast items on the menu, Jemme is all about long, elegant lunches in rococo-accented – and heavily air-conned – surrounds. Think exquisite plates and fine wine.

FRUIT MARKET *Market* $

cnr Jl Raya Kerobokan & Jl Gunung Tangkuban Perahu; 🕐 7am-7pm

Bali's numerous climate zones (hot and humid near the ocean, cool and dry up the volcano slopes) mean that pretty much any fruit or vegetable can be grown within the island's small confines. Look for the full range at the many vendor tables here, including odd-ball fruits you'll have never seen before (try a nubby mangosteen).

SARDINE *Seafood* $$$

☎ 0361-738202; Jl Petitenget 21;
🕐 Tue-Sun

Seafood fresh from the famous Jimbaran market is the star at this elegant yet intimate, casual yet stylish restaurant in a beautiful bamboo pavilion. Open-air tables

KEROBOKAN 'NIGHTLIFE'

Kerobokan hides behind its villas' walls at night, although what's behind these walls may surprise. On any night there's a few private parties going on that are a bit bigger than your average kegger in a backyard. Many feature top DJs and an attitude-heavy list of visiting (self-professed) celebrities and the like. On occasion the uninvited guests turn up in the form of police who invariably make a few arrests for drugs. Getting an invite to one of these soirees is rather elusive but bear in mind that many past guests have ended up at the Kerobokan Jail with Bali's most notable inmate: Australian Schapelle Corby.

overlook a private rice field that is patrolled by Sardine's own flock of ducks. The inventive bar is a must.

SARONG *Fusion* $$

☎ 0361-737809; www.sarongbali.com;
Jl Petitenget 19X; 🕐 noon-10pm

The food is almost as magical as the setting at this top-end, high-concept restaurant. Largely open to the evening breezes, the dining room has plush furniture and gleaming place settings that twinkle in the candlelight. But opt for tables out the back where you can let the stars do the twinkling. The food spans the globe; small plates are popular with those wishing to pace an evening enjoying the commodious bar.

REGIONS

KEROBOKAN

V

🍴 WAROENG BONITA
Indonesian $$

☎ **0361-731918; www.bonitabali.com; Jl Petitenget 2000X**

Balinese dishes such as *ikan rica-rica* (fresh fish in a spicy green-chilli sauce) are the specialities at this cute little place with tables set out under the trees. There's a breezy style that attracts people every night but on certain nights Bonita positively heaves because of the drag shows starring everyone from visiting queens to the busboy.

BEYOND KEROBOKAN

Northwest of Kerobokan are two beach areas popular with surfers and others looking for something a little different from the tourist crowds in Seminyak and the south. **Canggu Beach** is quiet on weekdays except for a few surfers who find reliable breaks through the year. Another 500m west along the shore is **Echo Beach**. Here there are popular surfer cafes and the **Beach House** (☎ 0361-738471; Jl Pura Batu Mejan), a slightly upmarket cafe open to the pounding surf. On Sundays expats flock here for a sunset barbecue.

Down, down, down from the lip – it's a great surf at Canggu Beach

WARUNG BATAVIA
Indonesian $
☎ 0361-731641; Jl Raya Kerobokan;
⏱ 10am-4pm

This slightly upmarket place on a busy road has a big choice of excellent, authentic Indonesian dishes. New creations stream forth from the kitchen throughout the middle of the day. Grab a quiet table at the back.

WARUNG GOSSIP
Indonesian $
☎ 0817-970 3209; Jl Pengubengan Kauh; ⏱ 11am-4pm

About 1km north of the jail, this popular warung serves top-notch versions of Balinese staples like satays in many forms. Get a plate, tell the staff what you'd like and soon you'll be enjoying a fine lunch at one of the shady tables. Many of the ingredients come from a nearby organic farmers market.

WARUNG KOLEGA
Indonesian $
☎ 0852-3794 9778; Jl Petitenget 98A;
⏱ 9am-5pm

This classic warung in the heart of Kerobokan makes no concessions to modern notions: the foods come out for lunch and if you come late (say after 2pm), the choices are cold or nonexistent. Quality is tops and dishes are spiced close to Balinese standards (think volcanic, like the island).

WARUNG SULAWESI
Indonesian $
Jl Petitenget; ⏱ 11am-4pm

Although seemingly upscale, Kerobokan is blessed with many a fine place for a local meal. Here you'll find a table in a quiet family compound and enjoy fresh Balinese and Indonesian food served in classic warung style. Choose a rice, then pick from a captivating array of dishes that are always at their peak at noon. The long beans – yum!

>JIMBARAN

For many, Jimbaran means a wonderful grilled seafood dinner overlooking the serene bay from tables on the sand. At the best places, the fish is soaked in a garlic and lime marinade, then doused with chilli and oil while it's grilling over coconut husks. At night you can't see for the thick clouds of smoke from the coals. But you can hear the roaming bands, who perform tunes from the 'I've got to be me' playlist. Many people actually join in. There are three distinct groups of seafood warung, each with its own personality as outlined in the Eat section (p64). By day, Jimbaran has two markets that bustle with business as Bali's rich stocks of fish, fruits and vegetables are bought and sold.

JIMBARAN

◉ SEE

⌂ SHOP

⦿ EAT

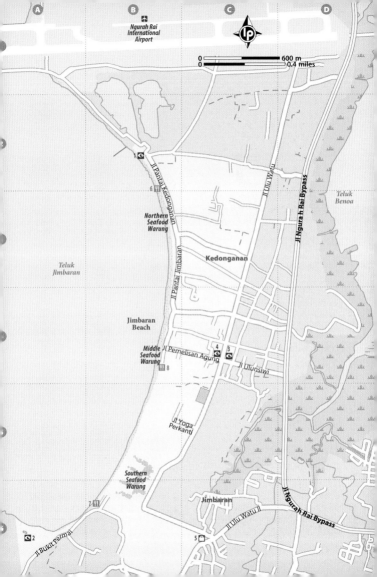

👁 SEE

👁 FISH MARKET

Jimbaran Beach; 🕑 **6am-1pm**
A popular morning stop on Bukit Peninsula ambles is this smelly, lively and frenetic fish market – just watch where you step. Brightly painted boats bob along the shore while huge cases of everything from small sardines to fearsome langoustines are hawked. The action is fast and furious.

👁 GANEESHA GALLERY

☎ **0361-701010; www.fourseasons.com; Four Seasons Jimbaran Bay**
This small but elegant gallery is part of the lavish Four Seasons compound. It has exhibitions by international artists and is worth a visit – walk south along the beach.

👁 MORNING MARKET

Jl Ulu Watu; 🕑 **6am-noon**
This is one of the best markets in Bali for a visit because: a) it's compact so you can see a lot without wandering forever; b) local chefs swear by the quality of the fruits and vegetables (ever seen a cabbage that big?); and c) they're used to tourists tromping about.

👁 PURA ULUN SIWI

Jl Ulu Watu
Across from the morning market, this ebony-hued temple from the 18th century is a snoozy place

AIRPORT DIVISIONS

The long runway at the airport effectively cuts off the Bukit Peninsula from the rest of Bali but for many it's not long enough. A longer runway would mean planes could fly nonstop to Europe, instead of stopping for fuel in Singapore or Jakarta as now. But opponents decry any more damage to the already mangled mangroves. And extending over the road is out of the question as tunnels are a cultural taboo.

until it explodes with life, offerings, incense and more on a holy day.

🛍 SHOP

🛍 JENGGALA KERAMIK BALI

Ceramics
☎ **0361-703310; Jl Ulu Watu II;** 🕑 **9am-6pm**
This modern warehouse showcases beautiful ceramic homewares that are a favourite Balinese purchase. There's a viewing area where you can watch production, and a cafe. Ceramic courses are available for adults and children.

🍴 EAT

🍴 GANESHA PUDAK CAFE

Seafood $$
☎ **0813-3855 3800; Jl Pantai Kedonganan**
The longest row of seafood restaurants is just south of the fish market. This is where a taxi will take you if you don't specify otherwise.

Most of these places are like this one: restaurant-like with tables inside and out on the immaculate raked sand. Call for free transport to/from much of the south.

TEBA MEGA CAFE
Seafood $$
☎ 0817-346068; off Jl Bukit Permai

The southern seafood warung are just north of the Four Seasons Jimbaran Bay. In many ways the warung are like the three bears: this group is not as formal as the northern group, not as rickety as the middle group – they are just right. There's a parking area off Jl Bukit Permai, and the beach here is well groomed with nice trees. Call for transport. Teba is the favourite of many long-term Bali expats.

WARUNG BAMBOO
Seafood $$
☎ 0361-702188; off Jl Pantai Jimbaran

The middle seafood warung are a compact group just south of

Cooked perfectly at a seafood warung, Jimbaran

Jl Pantai Jimbaran and Jl Pemelisan Agung junction. They are simple affairs, with old-fashioned thatched roofs and open sides. The beach is a little more natural, with the fishing boats up on the sand. Warung Bamboo is slightly more appealing than its neighbours, all of which have a certain raffish charm.

HOW MUCH IS THAT FISHY IN THE TANK?

Jimbaran's seafood warung draw tourists from across the south. The three groups of seafood warung do fresh barbecued seafood every evening (and noon at many). The open-sided affairs are right by the beach and perfect for enjoying sea breezes and sunsets. Tables and chairs are set up on the sand almost to the water's edge.

The usual deal is to select your seafood fresh from iced displays or tanks and pay according to weight. Expect to pay around 50,000Rp per 100g for live lobster, 20,000Rp to 30,000Rp for prawns, and 9000Rp for fish, squid and clams. Prices are open to negotiation and the accuracy of the scales is a joke among locals.

>ULU WATU & AROUND

When surfers go to heaven, many find themselves in this southwest corner of the Bukit Peninsula. Here world-famous surf breaks proceed down the coast like a perfect set of waves. Bingen, Impossibles and Padang are just some of the breaks that draw board riders from across the world. The absolute cream of the bunch is the namesake, Ulu Watu, which combines seven different breaks you access through a cave. Nonsurfers find little beaches at the base of the huge cliffs all along this rugged swath of coast. There's a range of low-key accommodation for everyone from surfers to honeymooners. And no visit is complete without a visit to the eponymous temple. Although the surf is ceaseless, the whole area is snoozy at night: the surfers party in Kuta.

ULU WATU & AROUND

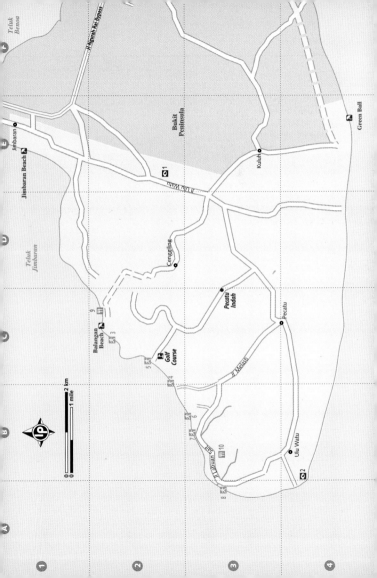

SEE

GARUDA WISNU KENCANA CULTURAL PARK

☎ 0361-703603; admission 15,000Rp, parking 5000Rp; ⏰ 8am-6pm; 👶

This yet-to-be-completed huge cultural park is meant to be home to a 66m-high statue of Garuda. In turn the statue will be erected on top of a shopping and gallery complex, for a total height of 146m, forming the biggest and highest statue in the world. Or so they say. So far the head's done – it's a biggie – and the landscaping is ace. But the other 140m still has a ways to go. It's worth stopping here on your way to Ulu Watu just for the fab views. If it's a clear day and you can see the volcanoes, you can't do better on the island.

PURA LUHUR ULU WATU

admission 3000Rp, incl sarong & sash rental, parking 1000Rp; ⏰ 8am-7pm

One of several important temples to the spirits of the sea along the south coast of Bali, Pura Luhur Ulu

Stone sentry at Pura Luhur Ulu Watu

Watu was established in the 11th century. The temple is perched precariously on the southwestern tip of the peninsula, atop sheer cliffs that drop straight into the pounding surf. You enter through an unusual arched gateway flanked by statues of Ganesha. Only Hindu worshippers can enter the small inner temple. But the real attraction is the location: the views out to sea seem to reach Africa (okay, Madagascar).

DAMN MONKEYS

Pura Luhur Ulu Watu is home to scores of grey monkeys. They're greedy little buggers: when they're not energetically fornicating they snatch sunglasses, handbags, hats and anything else within reach. Of course if you want to start a riot, show them your banana...

DO

BALANGAN

Go through the growing Pecatu Indah development and follow the road around to the right past

A TROVE OF COVES

Starting just south of Jimbaran, the rocky cliffs of the west coast of the Bukit Peninsula are scalloped out with a series of white-sand beaches in little coves. Most are named for the surf spots off-shore, such as hard-to-reach **Balangan Beach** (opposite). But once at this idyllic little spot, you'll decide the twisting 6km drive from the main Ulu Watu road was worth it. Little surfer cafes perch over the sands, and for a few dollars you can rent a lounger and soak up the sun, views and cold Bintangs. Others worth noting are **Bingin** and **Padang Padang** (below).

Dreamland to reach Balangan. There's a nice terraced area below the cliffs with a small temple and a couple of surfer cafes. The views are stunning up and down the coast. Balangan's surf break is a fast left over a shallow reef, unsurfable at low tide and good at midtide with anything over a 4ft swell; with an 8ft swell, this can be one of the classic waves.

🏃 BINGIN

Look for a road going to the right about 2km after you've taken the north fork at the village of Pecatu. A thicket of signs announce cheap surfer crash pads, quiet little cliffside resorts and impossibly expensive villas. Follow the dirt track back and eventually you'll reach a parking area with a good

path down to the tiny beach. Sheer cliffs soar above you while surfers fly over the waves in front of you. The waves are best at midtide with a 6ft swell, when short but perfect left-hand barrels are formed.

🏃 DREAMLAND

You have to go through the Pecatu Indah development to reach this sad spot. But the waves are still here and if you can avoid the construction, there's excellent surfing. At low 5ft swell, this solid peak offers a short, sharp right and a longer more tubular left.

🏃 IMPOSSIBLES

Just north of Padang Padang, this outside reef break has three shifting peaks with fast left-hand tube sections that can join up if the conditions are perfect (low tide, 5ft swell), but don't stay on for too long, or you'll run out of water. It is easily reached from Bingin.

🏃 PADANG PADANG

Several upmarket resorts crowd the clifftop overlooking this famous break. There's not much of a beach, so you're either surfing or watching here. Just 'Padang' for short, this super-shallow, left-hand reef break is just north of Pura Luhur Ulu Watu. If you can't surf tubes, backhand or forehand, don't go out: Padang is a tube.

REGIONS

ULU WATU & AROUND

BEATING ULU WATU

Observe where other surfers paddle out and follow them. If you are in doubt, ask someone. It is better having some knowledge than none at all. When the swell is bigger you will be swept to your right from the cave. Don't panic, it is an easy matter to paddle around the white water from down along the cliff. Coming back in you have to aim for the cave. When the swell is bigger, come from the southern side of the cave as the current runs to the north. If you miss the cave, paddle out again and repeat the procedure.

Many have compared it to a washing machine: it's not a spot for the faint-hearted.

⚑ ULU WATU

When the surf at Kuta Beach is 5ft to 6ft, Ulu Watu, the most famous surfing break in Bali, will be 6ft to 8ft with bigger sets. It is just about a kilometre north of Pura Luhur Ulu Watu; look for the packs of scooters equipped with surfboard racks. There are a few surfer cafes and warung out here, as well as lots of local guys ready to wax your board or fix that ding. And as if the amazing waves here weren't enough (there are seven different breaks), how you get into the water is an adventure in itself. You follow a rocky path down the cliff face and into a cave then paddle out.

Padang Padang (p69) – or just Padang for short – not for the faint-hearted

🍴 EAT

🍴 NASA CAFÉ *Beach Cafe* $

☎ 0818-0533 9118; Balangan Beach
Rickety bamboo supports a
lounging/drinking area where
the view through the tufted palm
leaves is impossibly blue water
streaked with white surf. Simple
food, simple rooms and simple fun
rule here.

🍴 YEYE'S WARUNG *Cafe* $$

Jl Labuan Sait
A gathering point away from the
cliffs at Padang Padang, Yeye's has
an easy going ambience, cheapish
beers and tasty Indonesian, Western and vegetarian food. Many
gather at night for the pizza.

⭐ PLAY

⭐ KECAK DANCE
Traditional Dance
**Pura Luhur Ulu Watu; admission
70,000Rp; ☀ sunset; ♿**
Although the performance
obviously caters for tourists,
the gorgeous setting in a small
amphitheatre in a leafy part of the
temple grounds makes it one of
the more delightful on the island.
The views out to sea are as inspir-
ing as the dance.

>NUSA DUA & TANJUNG BENOA

Popular with families and holidaymakers who love vast resorts, Nusa Dua seems far removed from Bali. In fact its huge beachside hotels and their hundreds of rooms could be anywhere in the world. It's a gated enclave where weeds – like uninvited locals – are marked for removal. Just to the north, slightly tatty Tanjung Benoa has the big beach resort vibe without the artificial gloss. An offshore reef protects the long strand of beaches here. Waves are but mere ripples. During the day, the northern end of the peninsula pulses with the shrieks of tourists enjoying all manner of watersports.

NUSA DUA & TANJUNG BENOA

🄲 SEE
Chinese Buddhist
 Temple 1 B1
Hindu Temple ....(see 1)
Mosque ....(see 1)
Pasifika Museum 2 C5

🄳 DO
Amanusa Spa 3 B6
Bali Golf & Country
 Club 4 C6
Benoa Marine
 Recreation 5 B2
Bumbu Bali Cooking
 School ....(see 7)

🄲 SHOP
Bali Collection 6 C5

🄴 EAT
Bumbu Bali 7 B3
Tao 8 B2
Warung Dobiel 9 B5

A

B

C

D

1

Jl Pratama   1

**Tanjung
Benoa**

5

8

2

*Tanjung
Benoa*

3

7

Jl Pratama

Selat Badung

4

Jl Nguruh Rai Bypass

Jl Pratama Raya

Beach Promenade

5

Jl Raya Bvalu Ungasan

Bualu

Jl Srikandi   9

2

6

**Nusa
Dua**

6

Jl Raya Bvalu Ungasan

Pantai
Mengiat

4

3

**Bali Golf &
Country
Club**

0 ———— 1 km
0 ———— 0.5 miles

👁 SEE

👁 BEACH PROMENADE

One of the nicest features of Nusa Dua is the 5km-long beach promenade that stretches the length of the resort and continues north along much of the beach in Tanjung Benoa. Not only is it a good stroll at any time but it also makes it easy to sample the pleasures of the other beachside resorts. The walk is paved for most of its length.

👁 PASIFIKA MUSUEM

☎ 0361-774559; Bali Collection, Block P, Nusa Dua; admission 60,000Rp; 🕙 10am-6pm

This grand new museum suffers from the same visitor neglect as the rest of the Bali Collection (see Shop, opposite). Good! You'll likely have the place to yourself. Several centuries of art from cultures around the Pacific Ocean are displayed. The influential wave of European artists that throve in Bali in the early 20th century is well represented.

FINDING FAITH

The fishing port of Benoa is one of Bali's multidenominational corners, with an interesting **Chinese Buddhist temple**, a **mosque** and a **Hindu temple** within 100m. It's an engaging little fishing town that makes for a good stroll.

🏃 DO

🏃 AMANUSA SPA

☎ 0361-772333; www.amanresorts .com; Nusa Dua; massage from US$50

The vaunted Amanusa Resort sets itself apart from Nusa's huge hotels with personal service, especially at its spa. Balinese and Swedish are among the massage techniques on offer, spa products are organic and a Reiki master is ready to 'redress energy imbalances'.

🏃 BALI GOLF & COUNTRY CLUB

☎ 0361-771791; www.baligolfandcoun tryclub.com; Nusa Dua; green fees US$165

Of course Nusa has an 18-hole course with all the amenities one

Tropical greens at Bali Golf & Country Club

THRILLS & SPILLS

Getting people wet is big business in Tanjung Benoa. Scores of operators put the hard sell on busloads of tourists brought in for a day on the water. As if by magic, all operators have similar prices. If you're an independent traveller, show up after 11am and you'll probably be able to cut a deal.

Among the offerings:

> **Banana-boat rides** (US$25 per 15 minutes) Wild rides for two as you try to maintain your grip on the inflatable fruit over the waves.
> **Jet-skiing** (US$25 per 15 minutes) Big with people who like to go fast and belch smoke.
> **Parasailing** (US$25 per ride) Popular; you float above the water while towed by a speedboat.

would expect. Lots of condos are going up along the fairways.

⚓ BENOA MARINE RECREATION
☎ 0361-771757; Jl Pratama, Tanjung Benoa

One of many watersport centres along the beach in Tanjung Benoa, BMR has a slightly more slick operation than the others but all rumble in the mornings as the buses pull in with day-tripping groups.

⚓ BUMBU BALI COOKING SCHOOL
☎ 0361-774502; www.balifoods.com; Jl Pratama, Tanjung Benoa; course US$80; ⏲ 6am-3pm

Heinz Von Holzen runs this much-lauded cooking school that strives to get to the roots of Balinese cooking. It starts with a 6am visit to Jimbaran's fish and morning markets, continues in

the large kitchen and finishes with lunch.

🛍 SHOP
🛍 BALI COLLECTION *Mall*
☎ 0361-771662; www.bali-collection .com; Nusa Dua

The shopping centre for Nusa Dua is a bit of a dud. And that's not for want of trying. Every major shop in Bali has an outlet here and there's a stylish Sogo department store direct from Tokyo. Maybe the crowds are down because tight security dissuades all but resort guests from wandering the wide, muzak-serenaded breezeways.

🍴 EAT
🍴 BUMBU BALI *Balinese* $$
☎ 0361-774502; Jl Pratama, Tanjung Benoa; ⏲ noon-9pm

Long-time resident and cookbook author Heinz von Holzen, his wife

Adyus Suyadnya
Driver/tour guide

What's your family like? My father is a rice farmer as was his father. Like it traditionally has been for the Balinese, rice was at the centre of their lives. **Is rice the centre of your life?** As a child I worked in our family fields. We could drink the water that flowed through the terraces. Now you can't and modern life means that you need more money than you get just farming. **Do you miss working with rice?** No. I have been driving visitors for many years and my motto is 'see the real Bali'. We go to the beautiful fields around Ubud and in the east and I can explain how it is part of our lives. **And your future?** Rice means you don't worry. No matter what happens, you can pray to God and use your hands and feet to grow rice.

Puji and an enthusiastic staff serve exquisitely flavoured dishes at this superb restaurant. Many diners opt for one of several set menus (from 210,000Rp). The *rijstaffel* shows the range of cooking in the kitchen from satays served on their own little coconut husk grill to the tender *be celeng base manis* (pork in sweet soy sauce) with a dozen more courses in between.

🍴 TAO *Asian* $$
☎ 0361-772902; www.taobali.com; Jl Pratama 96, Tanjung Benoa; 🚼

On its own swath of pure-white sand, Tao is one of the few options for a leisurely lunch right by the beach in Tanjung Benoa. Although it is part of the Ramada Resort, the hotel is across the street and Tao avoids the 'sign-for-it' vibe. A large curling pool wends between the tables. The food is an eclectic mix of Asian (but a club sandwich awaits philistines).

🍴 WARUNG DOBIEL
Balinese $
Jl Sri Kandi, Nusa Dua; ⏱ 10am-3pm

A bit of authentic joy amid the bland streets of Nusa, this warung

Even the barbecue is stylish at Bumbu Bali (p75)

celebrates pork. And what pork it is! The succulent pork satay is marinated for hours before it's grilled. The pork soup is the perfect taste-bud awakener, while the jackfruit is redolent with spices. Diners perch on stools and share tables.

REGIONS

NUSA DUA & TANJUNG BENOA

>SANUR

The first Westerners to make their homes in Bali (other than Dutch colonial bureaucrats) did so around Sanur over 100 years ago. It's easy to see why: there's a long beach protected by reefs, plenty of shady palm trees overhead and cool breezes off the ocean. Today these charms still apply. Sure Sanur has a bit of a snoozy rep, but those in the know scoff at this. It def-initely doesn't have the mania of Kuta but Sanur's spine, Jl Tamblingan, is lined with bars, cafes and shops. And while its serene beaches are as family-friendly as Nusa Dua's, they lack Nusa's artifice. Staying here is like, well, staying in Bali. Plus Sanur has an unbeatable location that's close to everything else: the natural beaches to the east, Ubud to the north, and the perils and pleasures of Kuta and Seminyak to the west.

SANUR

◎ SEE
Museum Le Mayeur **1** C1

🏃 DO
Boats to Nusa
   Lembongan **2** C1
Crystal Divers **3** C4
Jamu Traditional Spa **4** C3
Surya Water Sports **5** C5

🏠 SHOP
Gudang Keramic **6** C4
Hardy's **7** C4
Organic Market.............(see 6)
Red Camelia **8** C4

🍴 EAT
Bonsai Cafe **9** D3
Café Batu Jimbar **10** C4

Café Smorgås **11** C4
Mama Putu's **12** B6
Massimo **13** C5
Porch Café **14** C3
Sari Bundo **15** B5

🍸 DRINK
Café Billiard **16** C5
Cat & Fiddle **17** B6
Kalimantan **18** C2

Jl Hang Tuah

To Bali Orchid
Garden (3km)

To Nusa
Lembongan
(18km)

Jl Danau Bratan

Jl Danau Buyan

Jl Segara Ayu

Jl Danau Tondano

18

Jl Pantai Sindhu

Jl Danau Tamblingan

14

Jl Pantai
Karang

8

3
7

16

Jl Ngurah Rai (Bypass Rd)

Jl Tirtanadi

Jl Duyung

5

Selat
Badung

16

13

15

Jl Danau Poso

Jl Kesumasari

17

Jl Mertasari

0   600 m
0   0.4 miles

👁 SEE

👁 BEACHFRONT WALK

Sanur's beachfront walk was the first in Bali and has been delighting locals and visitors alike from day one. Over 4km long, it follows the sand south and curves to the west past resorts, beachfront cafes, wooden fishing boats under repair and quite a few elegant old villas built decades ago by the wealthy expats who fell under Bali's spell. While you stroll, look out across the water to Nusa Penida.

👁 MUSEUM LE MAYEUR

☎ 0361-286201; adult/child 2000/1000Rp; ⏲ 7.30am-3.30pm

More than 90 works by Le Mayeur (see boxed text, opposite) are on display in his old compound on the beach at the north end of Sanur's seafront. Paintings from his early period in Bali are romantic depictions of daily life and beautiful Balinese women. The works from the 1950s show the vibrant colours that later became popular with young Balinese artists.

👁 BALI ORCHID GARDEN

☎ 0361-466010; Jl Bypass Tohpati; admission 50,000Rp; ⏲ 8am-6pm

Given Bali's warm weather and rich volcanic soil, no one should be surprised that orchids thrive here. Fans of the delicate plant will love every

Silhouetted at sunrise on the beach at Sanur

MAKING BEAUTY BEAUTIFUL

Belgian artist Adrien Jean Le Mayeur de Merpes (1880–1958) arrived in Bali in 1932. Three years later he met and married the beautiful Legong dancer Ni Polok, when she was just 15. They lived in the beachfront compound that now houses the museum. The main house must have been delightful – a peaceful and elegant home filled with art and antiques right by the tranquil beach. After Le Mayeur's death, Ni Polok lived here until she died in 1985. The house is an interesting example of Balinese-style architecture – notice the beautifully carved window shutters that recount the story of Rama and Sita from the *Ramayana*. Also look for the hauntingly lovely black-and-white photos of Ni Polok.

display; others will enjoy the back areas, which have a wild tropical feel. The gardens are 3km north of Sanur along Jl Ngurah Rai just past the major intersection with the coast road, Jl Bypass Tohpati.

🏃 DO
CRYSTAL DIVERS
☎ 0361-286737; www.crystal-divers.com; Jl Danau Tamblingan 168; lessons from US$60

This slick diving operation has its own hotel and a large diving pool right outside the office. Recommended for beginners, the shop offers a long list of courses, including PADI open-water for US$425.

JAMU TRADITIONAL SPA
☎ 0361-286595; www.jamutraditionalspa.com; Jl Tamblingan 41; massage from US$45

The beautifully carved teak and stone entry sets the mood at this gracious spa, which offers a range of treatments including a popular Earth Essence Bust Treatment and a Kemiri Nut Scrub. Can't you just feel the 'ahhhhhhhh'?

🏃 SURYA WATER SPORTS
☎ 0361-287956; Jl Duyung 10; ⏱ 9am-5pm; 🚹

One of several watersports operations along the beach, Surya is the largest. You can go parasailing (US$15 per ride), snorkelling by boat (US$30, two hours), windsurfing (US$25, one hour) or rent a kayak and paddle the smooth waters (US$5 per hour).

🛍 SHOP
GUDANG KERAMIK
Ceramics
☎ 0361-289363; Jl Tamblingan

This is a real find. It's an outlet store for the highly regarded Jenggala Keramik Bali in Jimbaran (see p64). Prices are amazing and what's called 'seconds' here would be firsts everywhere else.

HARDY'S *Supermarket*
☎ 0361-285806; Jl Tamblingan 136;
🕑 8am-10pm

The Sanur outlet of this Bali chain has an entire floor of souvenirs. A lot of it is junk but there's some quality stuff such as teak carvings mixed in with everything else; the fixed prices are cheap. There's also a good-sized Periplus Bookshop here.

ORGANIC MARKET *Farmers Market*
Jl Danau Tamblingan; 🕑 10am-2pm Sun

Foodies take note: each week the Gudang Keramic parking lot is taken over by a host of Bali's best artisan and organic food producers. Treats abound.

RED CAMELIA *Clothing*
☎ 0361-270046; Jl Tamblingan 156

Ultra-comfortable womenswear in cotton and other relaxing fibres. Everything stretches right with you. Its custom tailoring has fans not just in Bali but among expats across the archipelago.

🍴 EAT

🍴 BONSAI CAFÉ *Cafe* $
☎ 0361-282908; Jl Tambligan 27

Although the menu is all beach-side standards (and good ones), the real reason to seek this place out is for the proof that the name is not notional: here are hundreds of bonsai trees in sizes from tiny to small.

🍴 CAFÉ BATU JIMBAR *Cafe-Bakery* $$
☎ 0361-287374; Jl Tamblingan 152; 👶

Popular locally for its fine food, this gem of a cafe has a shady wooden patio fronting an airy dining room. Succumb to the best banana smoothie in Bali, then let the luscious baked goods work their magic. A gourmet grocery adjoins.

🍴 CAFÉ SMORGÅS *Cafe* $
☎ 0361-289361; Jl Tamblingan; 👶

Set back from traffic, this sprightly place has nice wicker chairs outside and cool air-con inside. The menu has a healthy bent: try a detox drink (the opposite of fun for many...) and then live it up with quiche or carrot cake.

🍴 MAMA PUTU'S *Seafood* $
☎ 0361-270572; Jl Mertasari

A long-running seafood cafe where the menu changes depending on what's fresh (actually the menu stays the same but what's available changes…). Ask for extra garlic and don't miss the crisp coleslaw.

🍴 MASSIMO *Italian* $$
☎ 0361-288942; Jl Tamblingan 206

The interior is like an open-air Milan cafe, the outside like a

EXPAT HEAVEN

If the streets of Sanur seem to have more than their share of slow-moving – some would say 'contented' – Westerners, it is because Sanur is the real heart of Bali's expat community. Seminyak may get all the posers, but Sanur gets the ones with healthy retirement accounts. Many bars seem to have a few set-pieces (actually customers) perched daily on the same stool at the bar. Wait long enough and you may hear an aural variation of Sanur's common moniker 'Snore'.

One of the classic expat hangouts is the **Cat & Fiddle** (☎ 0361-282218; Jl Cemara 36), a faux-British pub with few walls in deference to the weather. For years the pub was even the home of the British Consulate (one person) until security concerns forced it into a compound.

Balinese garden – a delightful combo. Pasta, pizza and more are prepared with authentic Italian flair. No time for a meal? Nab some gelato from the counter up front.

PORCH CAFÉ *Cafe* $
☎ 0361-281682; Jl Tamblingan
Fronting Flashbacks, a charmer of a small hotel, this newish cafe is housed in a traditional wooden building replete with the name-sake porch. Snuggle up to a table out front or shut it all out in the air-con inside. The menu is a tasty mix of comfort food like burgers and freshly baked goods. Popular for breakfast; there's a long list of fresh juices.

SARI BUNDO *Indonesian* $
☎ 0361-281389; Jl Danau Poso; ☻ 24hr
This spotless padang-style shop-front is one of several at the south end of Sanur. Choose from an array of fresh and very spicy food. The curry chicken is a fiery treat that will have your tongue alternatively loving and hating you.

☒ DRINK

☒ CAFÉ BILLIARD *Bar*
☎ 0361-281215; Jl Danau Poso;
☻ noon-1am
Drawing a well-lubricated expat crowd, this open-air place keeps 'em happy with billiards and cheap Heineken. Many of the regulars feel more comfortable in the commodious wicker chairs than they do at home.

☒ KALIMANTAN *Bar*
☎ 0361-289291; Jl Pantai Sindhu 11
Also known as Borneo Bob's, this veteran boozer is one of many joints on this street popular with expats. It's a relaxed place with a palm-tree-shaded expanse and offers cheap drinks. For food, enjoy Mexican and Indonesian classics and steaks.

>DENPASAR

Bali's capital is often overlooked by visitors, despite being home to most of the island's people and covering much of South Bali. The streets can be chaotic and confusing, but there are also wide parks and boulevards that have a certain grandeur. And visitors will also see how far Bali has come from its rice-growing past: a fast-emerging middle class supports huge malls and other modern trappings. But traditional is here as well, from the island's main museums to its largest markets. And the growing prosperity supports an ever-expanding range of excellent – albeit simple – restaurants. If your idea of local food is shaped by some sodden mess of fried rice plopped onto your plate in Kuta, think again. Scores of places serve meals that are fresh, surprising and memorable. The locals wouldn't have it any other way.

DENPASAR

◎ SEE
Bajra Sandhi
   Monument **1** E4
Museum Negeri
   Propinsi Bali **2** C1
Pura Jagatnatha **3** C1

⌂ SHOP
Pasar Badung **4** B1
Pasar Kumbasari **5** B1

▯ EAT
Ayam Goreng Kalasan ...**6** E3
Cak Asm **7** D4

👁 SEE

🔲 MUSEUM NEGERI PROPINSI BALI

☎ 0361-222680; adult/child 5000/2500Rp; 🕙 8am-12.30pm Mon-Fri, 8am-3pm Sun

This large museum comprises several buildings and pavilions, including examples of the architecture of both the *puri* (palace) and *pura* (temple), with features such as a *candi bentar* (split gateway) and a *kulkul* (warning drum) tower. Among the old artefacts, look for the fine wood-and-cane carrying cases for transporting fighting cocks, and tiny carrying cases for fighting crickets. It's all a little dusty and never crowded, but it's an invaluable primer in Bali 101.

🔲 PURA JAGATNATHA
Jl Surapati

Next to the museum, the state temple is dedicated to the supreme god, Sanghyang Widi. Pause at the *padmasana* (shrine) made of white coral. It consists of an empty throne (symbolic of heaven) on top of the cosmic turtle and two *naga* (mythological serpents), which symbolise the foundation of the world.

🛍 SHOP

🔲 PASAR BADUNG *Market*
Jl Gajah Mada

Bali's largest market is busy in the morning and evening; it's a great place to browse and bargain. You'll find produce and food from all over the island, as well as easy-to-assemble temple offerings that are popular with working women.

🔲 PASAR KUMBASARI *Market*
Jl Gajah Mada

Handicrafts, a plethora of vibrant fabrics and costumes decorated with gold are just some of the goods at this huge market across the river from Pasar Badung. Plunge into the canyons of colour.

Surprises at Museum Negeri Propinsi Bali

THOSE DASTARDLY DUTCH

The huge **Bajra Sandhi Monument** (☎ 0361-264517; Jl Raya Puputan; adult/child 10,000/5000Rp; ☻ 9am-5pm) dominates what's already a big park in Renon. Inside this vaguely Borobodur-like structure are dioramas tracing Bali's history. Taking the name as a cue (it means: Monument to the Struggle of the People of Bali), you'll understand the jingoistic soap-opera quality of the dolls and their mayhem.

🍴 EAT

🍴 AYAM GORENG KALASAN
Indonesian $

☎ 0812-380 9934; Jl Cok Agung Trisna 6
The name here says it all: fried chicken (*ayam goreng*) named for a Javanese temple (Kalasan) in a region renowned for its fiery, crispy chicken. The version here falls off the bone on the way to the table; the meat is redolent with lemongrass from a long marinade prior to the plunge into boiling oil. There are several other excellent little warung in this strip.

🍴 CAK ASM *Balinese* $
☎ 0361-798 9388; Jl Tukad Gangga
No, the name of the place isn't the sound you make after eating here. If that were the case, this simple cafe would be named 'yum'. Join the government workers and students from the nearby university for superb dishes at rock-bottom prices. Order the *cumi cumi* (calamari) with *telor asin* sauce (a heavenly mixture of eggs and garlic). The resulting buttery, crispy goodness could well be the best dish you have while you're in Bali. And it will cost you less than US$1.

>UBUD

The phrase 'Ubud is the real Bali' is hackneyed to the point of cliché. But in many ways it *is* accurate. When you think about what really sets Bali apart from other beachy destinations, it is the culture, the rice fields and the inherent charm of the people – qualities that Ubud has in spades. By day a rice farmer leads his ducks in search of bugs, by night the eerie rhythm of the gamelan echoes in the distance; just some of the moments that capture hearts and have visitors pestering the front desk to extend their stay. Bali's rich artistic and dance traditions are also here to enjoy. And there's plenty of sybaritic spas and splendid restaurants to keep things from getting too high-minded. An Ubud highlight can be a walk across a verdurous rice field, witnessing a flawless dance or simply doing nothing at all.

UBUD

☺ SEE
Agung Rai Museum of
Art (ARMA) 1 D6
Blanco Renaissance
Museum 2 A4
Museum Puri Lukisan.....3 B3
Neka Art Museum 4 A1
Pura Marajan Agung ....(see 7)
Pura Taman Saraswati ...5 B3
Sacred Monkey Forest
Sanctuary 6 C5
Ubud Palace 7 C3

大 DO
ARMA............................(see 1)
Bali Bird Walks 8 A3
Pondok Pecak Library
& Learning Centre.......9 C4
Ubud Sari Health
Resort.......................10 B2
Yoga Barn 11 D5
Zen.............................12 C5

⌂ SHOP
Bali Cares.....................13 C4
Ganesha Bookshop......14 C4
Kertas Gingsir.............15 C4
Kou.............................16 C4
Macan Tidur.................17 B4
Namaste 18 C5
Pasar Seni....................19 C4
Pondok Bamboo..........20 C5
Produce Market..........(see 19)

⅋ EAT
Bali Buddha 21 C4
Café des Artistes 22 B4
Cafe Havana 23 C4
Casa Luna 24 B3
Coffee & Silver.............25 C5
Devilicious...................26 C4
Juice Ja Café 27 C4
Kafe Batan Waru ....(see 26)
Naughty Nuri's............28 A1
Three Monkeys............29 C5
Warung Ibu Oka 30 C3

☒ DRINK
Jazz Café......................31 D4
Napi Orti......................32 B4

★ PLAY
ARMA Open Stage ....(see 1)
Pura Dalem Ubud.........33 B3
Pura Taman
Saraswati ....(see 5)
Ubud Palace ....(see 7)
Ubud Tourist
Information...............34 B3

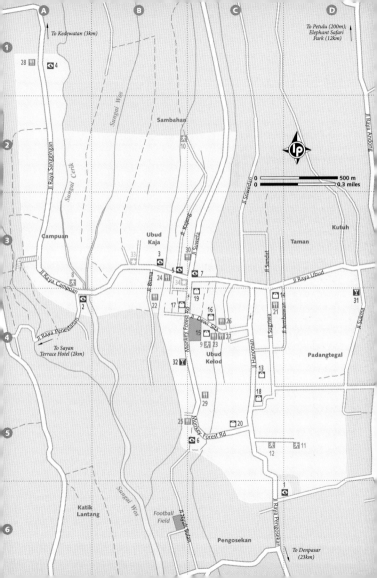

REGIONS

UBUD

SEE
AGUNG RAI MUSEUM OF ART
ARMA; ☎ 0361-976659; www. armamuseum.com; Jl Raya Pengosekan; admission 25,000Rp; ⏰ 9am-6pm
The impressive ARMA complex is the only place in Bali to see the haunting works by the influential German artist Walter Spies. It is housed in several traditional buildings set in gardens and features works by Lempad, Affandi, Sadali, Hofker, Bonnet and Le Mayeur. The collection is well labelled in English.

MUSEUM PURI LUKISAN
Museum of Fine Arts; ☎ 0361-975136; www.mpl-ubud.com; off Jl Raya Ubud; admission 20,000Rp; ⏰ 9am-5pm
Fine examples of all schools of Balinese art are shown at this excellent museum. It was in Ubud that the modern Balinese art movement started; where artists

BIRD BRAINS
Every evening at around 6 o'clock, thousands of big herons and egrets fly in to **Petulu**, just north of Ubud, squabbling over the prime perching places before settling into the trees beside the road, and becoming a minor tourist attraction. Villagers believe the birds bring good luck (as well as tourists), despite certain noxious leavings. Have a beer at the warung while enjoying the spectacle.

CHOOSING GALLERIES
Ubud is dotted with galleries – every street and lane seems to have a place exhibiting artwork for sale. They vary enormously in the choice and quality of items on display. Often you will find local artists in the most unusual places, including your guesthouse. The best way to deal with the plethora of choice is just keep browsing during your Ubud sojourn, gradually sorting out what seems special and what's replicated at every other stall.

first began to abandon purely religious themes and court subjects for scenes of everyday life. Just look at the lush composition of *Balinese Market* by Anak Agung Gde Sobrat to see the vibrancy of local painting.

NEKA ART MUSEUM
☎ 0361-975074; www.museumneka .com; Jl Raya Sanggingan; adult/child 40,000Rp/free; ⏰ 9am-5pm
This private museum has an excellent and diverse collection; it's the best place to learn about the development of painting in Bali. Various areas are named for some of Ubud's most renowned painters, including Arie Smit and I Gusti Nyoman Lempad. Also look for works by Louise Koke, Miguel Covarrubias, Rudolf Bonnet, Han Snel, the Australian Donald Friend and Antonio Blanco.

👁 PURA TAMAN SARASWATI
Ubud Water Palace; Jl Raya Ubud
An oasis in the heart of Ubud, waters from the temple at the rear feed a pond overflowing with iconic lotus blossoms. There's usually a few wannabe artists trying to capture the moment.

👁 SACRED MONKEY FOREST SANCTUARY
☎ 0361-971304; Monkey Forest Rd; adult/child 20,000/10,000Rp; ⏱ 8.30am-6pm
Besides three temples, this thick forest is inhabited by a band of grey-haired and greedy long-tailed Balinese macaques, which are nothing like the innocent-looking doe-eyed monkeys on the brochures. They are ever-vigilant for handouts from passing tourists.

👁 UBUD PALACE
cnr Jl Raya Ubud & Jl Suweta
Ubud's royal family still lives in this palace in the heart of town. In purely Balinese style, it has some ornate features and carving but is more comfortable family compound than grand retreat. Buck House it ain't, especially as you can wander around at will. Just to the north, **Pura Marajan Agung** (Jl Suweta) has one of the finest gates you'll find and is the private temple for the royal family.

Iconic lotus blossoms at Pura Taman Saraswati

ANTONIO BLANCO

The picture of Antonio Blanco mugging with Michael Jackson says it all, and the artist's flamboyant spirit is captured at the **Blanco Renaissance Museum** (☎ 0361-975502; Jl Raya Campuan; admission 50,000Rp; 🕙 9am-5pm). Blanco specialised in erotic art, illustrated poetry and playing the role of an eccentric artist à la Dali.

🏃 DO

🏃 ARMA

☎ 0361-976659; www.armamuseum .com; Jl Raya Pengosekan; classes US$25-55; 🕙 9am-6pm

The cultural powerhouse offers classes in painting, woodcarving and batik. Other courses include Balinese history, Hinduism and architecture.

🏃 BALI BIRD WALKS

☎ 0361-975009; tour US$35; 🕙 9am-12.30pm Tue, Fri, Sat & Sun

For the keen birdwatcher, this popular tour started by Victor Mason draws flocks. A gentle morning's walk will give you the opportunity to see maybe 30 of the 100 or so local species. The tours leave from the former Beggar's Bush Bar on Jl Raya Campuan.

🏃 UBUD SARI HEALTH RESORT

☎ 0361-974393; Jl Kajeng; 1hr massage from US$30; 🕙 8am-8pm

Function definitely trumps form at this no-nonsense spa, salon and hotel. The range of offerings is almost as copious as the poisons sure to be purged from your body.

🏃 YOGA BARN

☎ 0361-070992; www.balispirit.com; off Jl Raya Pengosekan; classes from 100,000Rp; 🕙 7am-8pm

Listen for the serenity leeching out from these trees back near a river valley. The name exactly describes what you'll find – although this barn never needs shovelling. A huge range of classes in yoga and life-affirming offshoots are held through the week.

RIDING JUMBO

Abandoned logging elephants from Sumatra have been given refuge in Bali (which never had its own elephants) at the **Elephant Safari Park** (☎ 0361-721480; www.baliadven turetours.com; adult/child US$16/8, rides US$45/32; 🕙 9am-5pm). Located in the wet highlands of Taro (12km north of Ubud), the park is home to almost 30 elephants that stoically provide rides to unstoic humans.

WALK IN PARADISE

The beauty of Sungai Ayung (River Ayung) is the focus of this outing, where you will walk below the luxury hotels built to take advantage of this lush, tropical river valley. Head west from Ubud across rice fields to Sayan. Look for the Sayan Terrace Hotel and follow the path down to the river. Following the rough trails north, along the eastern side of the river, you traverse steep slopes, cross paddy fields and penetrate thick, tropical jungle. After about 1.5km you'll reach the finishing point for many white-water rafting trips – a steep trail goes up to the main road at Kedewatan, where you can walk back to Ubud.

✈ ZEN

☎ 0361-970976; Jl Hanoman; 1hr massage 100,000Rp; ⏲ 9am-8pm

Down a little lane, this spa has a good reputation. It offers body scrubs, 90-minute *mandi lulur* (Javanese body scrubs) and a spice bath (160,000Rp), among myriad other pleasures.

🛍 SHOP

🛍 GANESHA BOOKSHOP

Bookshop

☎ 0361-970320; www.ganeshabooks bali.com; Jl Raya Ubud

Ubud's best bookshop has an amazing amount of stock jammed into a small space; an excellent selection of titles on Indonesian studies, travel, arts, music, fiction (including used titles) and maps. Good staff recommendations.

🛍 KERTAS GINGSIR *Paper*

☎ 0361-973030; Jl Dewi Sita

This place specialises in gorgeous and heavily textured papers hand-

made from banana, pineapple and taro plants. If you're into pulp, ask about factory visits.

🛍 KOU *Soaps*

☎ 0361-971905; Jl Dewi Sita

Luxurious handmade organic soaps made locally perfume your nose as you enter. Put one in your undies drawer and smell fine for weeks. The range is unlike that found in chain stores selling luxe soap.

🛍 MACAN TIDUR *Art & Antiques*

☎ 0361-977121; Monkey Forest Rd

Amid a string of trashy places selling tourist tat, this elegant store

UBUD'S LIBRARY

The **Pondok Pecak Library & Learning Centre** (☎ 0361-976194; Monkey Forest Rd; ⏲ 9am-5pm Mon-Sat, 1-5pm Sun), on the far side of the football field, is a relaxed place with a children's book section, a pleasant reading area on the roof, a lending library and a range of cultural and language courses on offer.

REGIONS

UBUD

stands out like Audrey Hepburn amid the Spice Girls. Silks, art, antiques and more are beautifully displayed in a lovely shop that will have you pondering your shipping options.

🗐 NAMASTE *New Age*
☎ **0361-796 9178; Jl Hanoman 64**
Just the place to buy a crystal to get your spiritual house in order, Namaste is a gem of a little store with a top range of New Age supplies. Incense, yoga mats, moody instrumental music – it's all here.

🗐 PASAR SENI *Souvenirs*
Art Market; Jl Raya Ubud
Many bus-bound tourists can feel trapped at this chaotic warren of stalls in the heart of Ubud. Clothing, sarongs, footwear and souvenirs of highly variable quality are sold at highly negotiable prices. Take time to look through the tat (not another carved penis

please!), as decent souvenirs include leather goods, batiks and baskets.

🗐 PONDOK BAMBOO
Musical Instruments
☎ **0361-974807; Monkey Forest Rd**
Hear the music of a thousand bamboo wind chimes at this shop owned by noted gamelan musician Nyoman Warsa. Gamelans in many forms are on offer and the master himself is ready to explain the workings. Ask about puppet and music performances you may be able to attend.

🗐 PRODUCE MARKET *Market*
Jl Raya Ubud; 🕐 **6am-1pm**
Hidden behind the euphemistically named art market is this real, working market (this is where your meals start), operating to a greater or lesser extent every day. Browse Bali's fab range of fresh foodstuffs.

🍴 EAT

🍴 BALI BUDDHA *Healthy* $
☎ **0361-976324; Jl Jembawan 1;** Ⓥ
This breezy upper-floor place offers a full range of vegetarian *jamu* (health tonics), salads, tofu curries, savoury crepes, pizzas and gelato. It has a comfy lounging area and is candlelit at night. On the ground floor a market sells organic fruit and vegetables,

---

CARING IN UBUD
Bali Cares (☎ 0361-981504; www .idepfoundation.org; Jl Hanoman 44) is a lovely shop selling goods to benefit several local and Indonesian charities. Items range from woodcarvings made from sustainable woods to paintings, handicrafts and other items produced by local people. The shop is an excellent resource for information on charitable and nonprofit groups.

Raw rice, shallots, tomatoes, garlic, ginger, onions and chillies – cooking up a storm, Bali-style

wondrous blueberry muffins, breads and cookies. The bulletin board is packed with idiosyncratic Ubud notices.

🍴 CAFÉ DES ARTISTES
Belgian $$

☎ **0361-972706; Jl Bisma 9X;**
🕙 **noon-midnight**

In a quiet and cultured perch up off Jl Raya Ubud, the popular (meaning book in high season) Café des Artistes serves Belgian-accented food, although the menu strays into France and Indonesia as well. There's also some amazing steaks. Local art is on display and the bar is refreshingly cultured.

🍴 CAFE HAVANA
Latin, Eclectic $$

☎ **0361-972973; Jl Dewi Sita**

All that's missing is Fidel. Actually, the decrepitude of its namesake city is also missing from this smart and stylish cafe on smart and stylish Dewi Sita. The menu boasts many a dish with Latin flair, such as tasty pork numbers, but expect surprises such as a crème brûlée oatmeal in the morning that simply astounds.

🍴 CASA LUNA *Indonesian* $$

☎ **0361-977409; Jl Raya Ubud**

Enjoy creative Indonesian-focused dishes like addictive bamboo skewers of minced seafood satay (try to

PIG ON A SPIT

Opposite Ubud Palace at **Warung Ibu Oka** (Jl Suweta; 11am-4pm) you'll see lunchtime crowds waiting for one thing: the eponymous Balinese-style roast suckling pig. Line up and find a place under the shelter for one of the best meals you'll have in Ubud. Order a *spesial* to get the best cut. Get there early to avoid the day-tripping bus tours.

pick out the dozen or so spices). Bread, pastries, cakes and more from its well-known bakery are also a must. The owner, Janet de Neefe, is the force behind the lauded Ubud Writers & Readers Festival.

🍴 COFFEE & SILVER *Cafe*　$
☎ 0361-975354; Monkey Forest Rd; 10am-midnight

Tapas and more substantial items make up the menu at this comfortable place with seating inside and out. Vintage photos of Ubud line the walls. Have a coffee and watch people strolling down to their fate with the monkeys in the forest.

🍴 DEVILICIOUS *Cafe*　$
☎ 0361-745972; Jl Goutama

Jl Goutama is a delightful street for a stroll and this cafe is one of the reasons why. Just wandering the narrow lane is like stepping back 30 years in Ubud and little

creative places like this cafe seem to appear like mushrooms after the rain. Look for theme nights such as Cajun Friday and Italian Tuesday.

🍴 JUICE JA CAFÉ *Cafe*　$
☎ 0361-971056; Jl Dewi Sita

Glass of spirulina? Dash of wheat grass with your papaya juice? Organic fruits and vegetables go into the food at this funky bakery-cafe. Little brochures explain the provenance of items like the organic cashew nuts. Enjoy the patio.

🍴 KAFE BATAN WARU
Indonesian　$$
☎ 0361-977528; Jl Dewi Sita

One of Ubud's best, this cafe serves consistently excellent Indonesian food. Tired of tired *mie gorengs* made from instant noodles? With noodles made fresh daily, this version celebrates a lost art. Western dishes include sandwiches and salads. Smoked duck *(bebek betutu)* and spit-roasted pig *(babi guling)* can be ordered in advance. Ask for a table on the small terrace that sits over a burbling stream; they are the pick of the house.

🍴 NAUGHTY NURI'S
Barbecue　$$
☎ 0361-977547; Jl Raya Sanggingan

This legendary expat hangout packs 'em in for grilled steaks,

Lili Molloy
Teenager in Ubud, fashion model, dedicated shopper

Where did you grow up? Right in Ubud, my mum is from Australia and owns shops, my father is from here. **Favourite things about Ubud?** The shopping and the art! Dewi Sita is one of the greatest streets for shopping. There are cool designers who have their shops right here; you can go in and talk to them. I also like art, and no matter which way you go in Ubud, somebody can give you lessons. **What's a good walk?** Pretty much anywhere here. I just wander the streets and see new things all the time. You can go out in the countryside where it's beautiful, but who wants to get sweaty? **And a favourite snack?** I wander around the produce market (p94). Nothing comes wrapped in plastic, instead you buy a mango – I love mango season! – and eat it there. I also like the rambutans and mangosteens.

REGIONS

UBUD

ribs and burgers. Thursday night grilled-tuna specials are ridiculously popular, making something of a party scene. Potent drinks fuel the fun.

🍴 THREE MONKEYS *Fusion* $$

☎ 0361-974830; Monkey Forest Rd
Have a passionfruit-crush cocktail and settle back amid the rice field's frog symphony. Add the glow of tiki torches for a magical effect. By day there are sandwiches, salads and gelato. At night there's a fusion menu of Asian classics (the prawn rolls are a must), pasta and steaks.

🍸 DRINK
🍸 JAZZ CAFÉ *Venue*

☎ 0361-976594; Jl Sukma 2; dishes 35,000-60,000Rp; ⏰ 5pm-midnight
Ubud's most popular nightspot (and that's not faint praise even though competition might be

lacking), Jazz Café offers a relaxed atmosphere in a charming garden that features coconut palms and ferns. The menu offers a range of good Asian fusion food and you can listen to live music from Tuesday to Saturday after 7.30pm. The cocktail list is long.

🍸 NAPI ORTI *Bar*

☎ 0361-970982; Monkey Forest Rd; drinks from 12,000Rp; ⏰ noon-late
This upstairs place is your best bet for a late-night drink. Get boozy under the hazy gaze of Jim Morrison and Sid Vicious.

⭐ PLAY

Ubud has cultural performances virtually every night. The venues vary, however, with some being easily walkable from the centre and others requiring a ride. In a week in Ubud you can see Kecak, Legong and Barong dances, *Mahabharata* and *Ramayana* ballets, *wayang kulit* puppets and gamelan orchestras. A few of our favourite venues follow. Costs range from 50,000Rp to 100,000Rp.

⭐ ARMA OPEN STAGE *Venue*

☎ 0361-976659; Jl Raya Pengosekan
The great cultural centre attracts some of the best troupes. It is part of the large cultural centre and hotel of the same name.

Beating out a synchronised rhythm – the magical sounds of a traditional gamelan orchestra

⭐ PURA DALEM UBUD *Venue*
Jl Raya Ubud
At the west end of Jl Raya Ubud, this open-air venue has a flamelit carved-stone backdrop. Watch for the Semara Ratih troupe.

⭐ PURA TAMAN SARASWATI *Venue*
Ubud Water Palace; Jl Raya Ubud
The beauty of the setting may distract you from the dancers, although at night you can't see the lily pads that are such an attraction by day.

⭐ UBUD PALACE *Venue*
Jl Raya Ubud
Performances are held here almost nightly against a beautiful backdrop in the palace compound, with the carvings highlighted by torches.

>EAST BALI

Some of the lushest land in Bali is found in the east. Ancient rice terraces spill down the sides of hills into wide river valleys. For a primer in just how 'green' green can be, take the road from Semarapura to Sidemen. Many people spend their holidays hiking the many trails in and around Sidemen. Along the coast, posh and more humble resorts are scattered along the hilly shore. Long beaches in the west give way to smaller hidden ones in the east. Padangbai is a port town with a funky feel while Semarapura has important relics from Bali's royal past. You can spend a day (it's an easy drive from Kuta or Sanur) or a week exploring East Bali.

EAST BALI

◉ SEE
Lebih Beach	1	B4
Padangbai	2	D3
Saba Beach	3	A4
Sidemen Road	4	C2
Taman Kertha Gosa	5	B3
Tenganan	6	E2

⚐ DO
Bali Safari & Marine Park	7	B4
Geko Dive	8	D3

⊪ EAT
Amankila Terrace	9	D2
Gianyar Babi Guleng	10	A3
Merta Sari	11	C3
Vincent's	12	E2

▼ DRINK
Ozone Café	13	D3

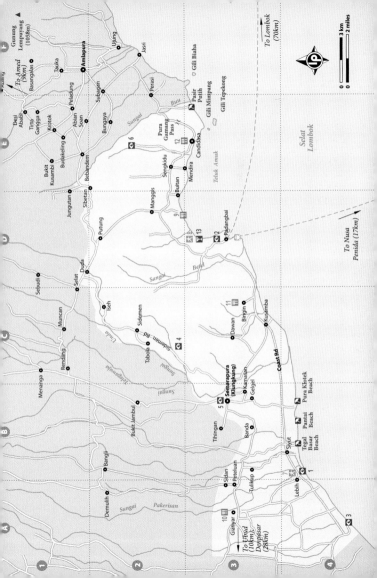

◉ SEE

◉ PADANGBAI

Bali's eastern port city makes a good base for exploration. You can relax on the beach with a beer while watching the Lombok ferry come and go or head just over a knoll to the light-sand Blue Lagoon Beach, which is a good place to snorkel. A couple of small temples, a modern market and a cool traveller vibe make this the pick of the towns in the east for an overnight stop.

◉ SIDEMEN ROAD

Sidemen has a spectacular location and the road that runs through it may be the most beautiful in Bali (start at Semarapura, end near Duda). There are many walks through the rice fields and streams in the multihued green valley that forms what could be an amphitheatre for the gods. Be ready to avert your eyes when you come upon villagers stoically bathing in the buff.

◉ TAMAN KERTHA GOSA

Semarapura; adult/child 12,000/6000Rp, parking 2000Rp; ⏱ 7am-6pm

When the Dewa Agung dynasty moved here in 1710, this palace was established. It was laid out as a large square, believed to be in the form of a mandala, with courtyards, gardens, pavilions and moats. Most of the original palace and grounds were destroyed by Dutch attacks

Spectacular Sidemen – green and glorious

in 1908 – the elaborately carved gateway on the south side of the square is all that remains of the palace itself. While wandering the gardens, save time for the good little museum. Semarapura is a busy market town and you can find scores of warung with fresh fare.

⊙ TENGANAN

Bali's oldest inhabitants are the Bali Aga people, who lead lives separate from Hindu Bali. Tenganan, their spiritual home, is surrounded by a wall, which protects the small village from outside influences. Not *all* outside influences mind you, as the Aga have found profits in accepting visitors. The most striking feature of Tenganan is its postcard-like beauty, with the green hills providing a serene backdrop. Happily residents are pretty low-key with visitors. You'll be gently offered exquisitely crafted baskets and artful *lontar* (specially prepared palm leaves) strips. Tenganan is 4km off the coast road just west of Candidasa.

⚐ DO

⚐ BALI SAFARI & MARINE PARK

☎ 0361-950000; www.balisafarimarine park.com; Prof Dr Ida Bagus Mantra Bypass; admission from US$12; ⏲ 9am-5pm

Kids love this animal theme park that is filled with critters whose species never set foot in Bali until their cage doors opened. Displays are large and naturalistic. A menu of extra-cost options includes camel and elephant rides. The vast park is north of Lebih Beach.

⚐ GEKO DIVE

☎ 0363-41516; www.gekodive.com; Jl Silayukti, Padangbai; two-tank dives US$70-120

Padangbai is one of East Bali's diving centres. You can dive the reefs near town or head further out to the superb sites around Nusas Lembongan and Penida. Geko Dive is a long-established operator and has a nice cafe across from the beach.

BALI'S EASTERN BEACHES

The busy coast road from Sanur going east has made it easy to get to large stretches of shore that were previously inaccessible. From north of Sanur the sand runs almost all the way to Kusamba. The grey sands are mostly empty and the surf is always treacherous. A couple of good choices are **Saba Beach**, which has a small temple, and **Lebih Beach**, which has sand filled with mica that sparkles with a billion points of light.

Further east there are a few nice beaches in and around Padangbai, while there are none at all at Candidasa owing to a disastrous decision to dynamite the reef to make cement. Elsewhere there are a few gorgeous tiny crescents of sand hidden by cliffs at the end of primitive tracks.

🍴 EAT

🍴 AMANKILA TERRACE

Fusion, Balinese $$$

☎ 0363-41333; www.amankila.com;
Manggis; 🕐 8am-5pm

One of Bali's finest hotels is hidden along the jutting cliffs about 5km beyond the Padangbai turn-off. The renowned architecture features three main swimming pools that step down to the sea in matching shades of a blue that doesn't seem real. Restaurant-wise, the superb Terrace is the more casual and has a creative menu showing global and local influences. Service vies with the view for your plaudits.

🍴 GIANYAR BABI GULENG

Balinese $

Gianyar; 🕐 7am-4pm

People come to Gianyar to sample the market food, like the *babi guling* (spit-roast pig stuffed with chilli, turmeric, garlic and ginger) for which the town is noted. Although scoring a zero for imagination in naming it, this open-air shopfront scores a 10 for its *babi*, which is first among much competition. It's on a tiny side street at the west end of the centre. Look for the large sign.

🍴 MERTA SARI *Indonesian* $$

Bingin; 🕐 10am-3pm

Follow the crowds of Balinese to this open-air pavilion that's famous for its *nasi campur*. This version of

the island's plate lunch includes juicy, pounded fish satay, a slightly sour, fragrant fish broth, fish steamed in banana leaves, snake beans in a fragrant tomato-peanut sauce and a fiery red sambal. Merta Sari is 300m north of the coast road in Bingin. Look for the signs.

🍴 VINCENT'S *Asian* $$

☎ 0363-41368; Jl Raya Candidasa,
Candidasa; Ⓥ

The best reason for stopping in Candidasa, Vincent's main room feels like the living room at your tasteful friend's holiday house. It's open, airy and inviting. A lovely rear garden with rattan lounge furniture is the real draw, however, as it's far from the roaring traffic on the main road. There's a plethora of artfully prepared Thai and vegie options, but the real stars are the Balinese dishes. It has a refined bar.

🍸 DRINK

🍸 OZONE CAFÉ *Bar*

☎ 0363-41501; Padangbai

This popular travellers' spot in the centre of town has more character than all the places in East Bali combined. Incomprehensible slogans painted on the wall (eg: Acting like a monkey when you see a nice girl is so important for you) set the tone. There's pizza, and patrons often provide music, with the quality decreasing through the night.

>FURTHER AFIELD

Water wonder – Air Terjun Gitgit near Lovina (p109)

NUSA LEMBONGAN

One of three islands just off the southern coast of East Bali, Nusa Lembongan is the beach escape for people ready to escape their Bali beach escape. Boats pull ashore at the tiny village of Jungubatu, where a long strand of white sand fronts reef-protected shallows in which locals grow seaweed used to, yes, thicken ice cream. Past the coral are surf breaks ready to lay waste to beginners. The name of one, Lacerations, says it all.

Reef life at Blue Corner off Nusa Lembongan's west coast

There are great diving possibilities around Nusa Lembongan and its much larger neighbour, the thinly populated Nusa Penida. Prime spots include a series of shallow and sheltered reefs. Expert divers enjoy demanding drift dives in the channel between Nusa Ceningan and Penida and the sheer drops along Penida. Large marine animals, including turtles, sharks, manta rays and the large (3m fin to fin) and unusual *mola-mola* (sunfish) are often seen. Good local dive shops on Lembongan include **World Diving** (☎ 081-2390 0686; www.world-diving.com). Snorkelling in mangroves rich with sea life and the close-in reefs is popular.

Even if you're not getting wet, the laid-back vibe is reason enough to visit Lembongan. The main beach is lined with simple guesthouses. After dark, nightlife bustles at funky hangouts such as **Scooby Doo Cafe**, where you can watch the sun set over Bali while sipping a cocktail. Overlooking the beach from a knoll just to the south are somewhat posher guesthouses. None is very large, and a crowd is when four people turn up at one of the cliffside cafes for a grilled seafood dinner.

Even more remote are the resorts at Mushroom Bay on the island's west end. The cove of blue water is postcard-perfect and there's not a phone or TV in sight to interrupt your idyll.

Don't be surprised if the days just melt away. Nusa Lembongan only has 7000 residents and much of the island is an expanse of coconut trees. The two tiny villages barely qualify as such. There are no cars, but simple lanes and a rugged path encircling much of the island allow you to explore a few beautiful and otherwise untrammelled beaches. Should sloth strike (likely) you can rent a motorbike. ATMs and other services don't exist; bring cash – and a good book.

INFORMATION

Location 17km east of Sanur
Getting there Boats leave from Sanur: the fastest way is by the appropriately named Scoot, which reaches the island in 30 minutes (departure times vary); fast public boats leave from the northern end of Sanur beach at various times and take less than an hour
Contact Scoot (☎ 0361-285522; www.scootcruise.com)
Costs Scoot adult/child return US$50/34; public boats 150,000Rp
When to go Year-round

AMED & TULAMBEN

These two towns on Bali's somewhat arid far-east coast have one thing in common: they exist in the shadow of Gunung Agung, Bali's revered but also potentially dangerous volcano. Lava from its disastrous 1963 eruption is much in evidence.

But they differ greatly in their appeal: **Tulamben** is devoted to diving by virtue of a wrecked ship right off its stone-strewn shore. **Amed**, on the other hand, is about having nothing to do at all.

Although this long thin strip of coast at the base of steep hills is generically called 'Amed', it is really a series of tiny fishing villages of which Amed is merely the first that most people encounter. Others include **Jemeluk**, **Lipah** and the butt of many a joke, **Aas**. Riding the road linking these villages you soon settle into an easy rhythm: the road dips down to a small cove with a beach enlivened by rows of polychromatic fishing boats, it then climbs to bluffs with views far out to sea before dipping down to the next town.

There are scores of little places to stay along the Amed coast. Your biggest decision is whether to opt for a beach or knoll location. Most have spas and many are specifically aimed at guests hoping to mix a little yoga or other enlightening pursuit with their holiday. There's few places to eat outside of hotels and even fewer shops. Mostly you come to the coast to do nothing at all.

Conversely, Tulamben is all about being active. The smallest grain of sand on the 'beach' is as large as your hand. There's no hiking and no place to shop. But there is the *Liberty,* a large wrecked WWII freighter a few minutes' swim directly from the shore. The dozen or so hotels here all have in-house dive operations and many people come here to get their diving certificate or for advanced classes. Diving – or snorkelling – the wreck is a doable day-trip from the south and Ubud.

INFORMATION

Location Amed is about 65km by the coast road from Sanur; Tulamben is 70km
Getting there Amed is about three hours' drive from the south; allow four hours for Tulamben
Costs Car rental US$30 per day; car with driver US$40 to US$50 per day
When to go Year-round

LOVINA & THE NORTH

With all the focus on south Bali, many people overlook the north. This wasn't always the case. In the steamship era, boats docked in the port town of **Singaraja** and visitors began their Bali adventure from the north. It was a good introduction as the regency of Singaraja has always been especially proud of being, well, Balinese. Some of the island's best dance and gamelan groups perfect their art in little villages across the region.

But few outsiders know this as most of these groups head south – like many of their job-seeking neighbours – to actually perform. Rather, visitors who make the journey to the north usually have only one destination in mind, the beach town of Lovina. Actually there's not much Lovina in this area, as it's really a long string of old fishing villages that have been christened with the generic moniker 'Lovina' by visitors over the years. Being Balinese, the locals have just gone along with it.

This kind of laissez-faire attitude is the perfect metaphor for all of 'Lovina'. It's a relaxed, mellow place that for much of the year borders on being snoozy. A long thin grey-sand beach links the fishing villages (where boats still make the journey out each day). It's lapped by some pretty relaxed waves – no surfing here. Guesthouses leaning towards the modest end are scattered about. A few relaxed bars support just enough nightlife to keep things interesting. Otherwise, as someone said, 'It's a fine place to work on my journal. If I kept a journal.'

Outside of Lovina and bustling, commercial Singaraja, north Bali is thinly populated; searching out remote temples and waterfalls is a great way to spend a day.

INFORMATION
Location Lovina is about 80km north of Kuta
Getting there Count on two hours up and over the mountains to Lovina; you can also take the coast road around either west or east and do it in four or five hours
Costs Car rental US$30 per day; car with driver US$40 to US$50 per day
When to go Year-round

MOUNTAINS

Volcanoes are the spine of Bali and for many they are the soul. Climbing the many roads that traverse Bali's mountains, you'll notice at some indefinable moment that palm trees have been replaced by pines and rice has given over to coffee and you'll realise that, yes, you are entering another world.

The steep slopes divide the broad plains of the south from the narrower strip of the north. And these peaks don't just loom large over the land; they also loom large over the Balinese. The island's 'Mother Mountain' **Gunung Agung** (3142m) is in the east. Often cloud-shrouded, it occasionally emits a puff of smoke or, worse, lava. Ascending this peak is a major accomplishment, with a stunning sunrise as a reward. **Ketut Uriada** (☎ 0812-364 6426) can arrange treks.

Mountain mist and silent prayer on Gunung Batur

Northwest is **Gunung Batur** (1717m). On a clear day from the edge of its double caldera there is the truly astonishing view of a large lake within, and yet another lunar-like cone of a volcano rising Matrushka-like beside the lake's blue waters. It's a spectacle that almost makes it possible to forget the hordes of obnoxious touts selling junk or hawking tours. Almost.

Further west in the **Danau Bratan** (Lake Bratan) area, dense forest covers a complex of long-dormant volcanic craters, interspersed with several lakes. The area is known for its sweet strawberries, which you can buy at cute little roadside cafes in and around **Bedugul** and **Candikuning**. Pause at the **Bali Botanical Gardens** (☎ 0368-21273; Candikuning; admission 7000Rp; ☽ 7am-6pm), a showplace garden boasting trees, flowers and orchids from across Indonesia. Or follow the faithful to **Pura Ulun Danu Bratan** (Candikuning; adult/child 10,000/5000Rp; ☽ tickets 7am-5pm, site 24hr), a Hindu-Buddhist temple of great importance that dates from the 17th century. It is dedicated to Dewi Danu, the goddess of the waters, and is actually built on small islands within the lake.

A small road following the crest of the mountains branches off the road to Singaraja and travels west through the mist-laden forests to **Munduk**. Here there's a dense landscape of waterfalls, jungle and coffee plantations. Visitors come to hike the lush hillsides while staying in small guesthouses, some dating back to colonial times. On clear days you'll have a panorama stretching down to the north coast. It can get chilly, so a stop at **Ngiring Ngewedang** (☎ 0828-365146; ☽ 10am-4pm), a coffee house 5km east of Munduk, is a must. The delicious brew is made from beans picked on the surrounding slopes.

INFORMATION
Location Towns are 30km to 40km from South Bali
Getting there Use the two main roads into the mountains from South Bali, plus some minor roads to make a fascinating circular day trip
Costs Car rental US$30 per day; car with driver US$40 to US$50 per day
When to go Year-round

I B Anom
Master carver of masks and wood and a teacher of his craft

Where do you work? Three generations of us carve in our family's compound. It's shady and we just sit outside and work. **What do you carve?** We do masks for ceremonies and performances. There are many different kinds. We start with cedar logs and cut them down to size for carving – that's the hard part, we try to get each other to do it. But we all like the carving. **How long to create a mask?** Usually about two weeks. You have to work with the wood and see what it will yield. When things are going well, you'll discover it's after 4am and there's light in the sky. **Have styles changed?** Balinese art – even that used for traditional occasions – is always changing and much depends on the artist. Paints and colours are much brighter than just a few years ago.

MENJANGAN ISLAND

'I kept getting water in my mouth because I was smiling so much,' said a friend. It's the closest we've ever come to hearing a complaint about the beautiful dive spots around Menjangan Island. Located within the boundaries of Bali's only national park, **Taman Nasional Bali Barat** (West Bali National Park), the island is renowned for its great mix of dive and snorkelling sites. The island is deserted, which helps keep the waters pristine.

Although a bit battered by nature and illegal fishing, the coral is in good shape. Lacy sea fans and various sponges provide both texture and hiding spots for small fish that form a colour chart for the sea. Like our friend, few can resist the silly charms of parrot and clown fish. Among larger creatures, you may see whales, whale sharks and manta rays gracefully swimming by.

Of the dozen or so named sites here, most are close to shore and suitable for snorkellers or diving novices. Venture a bit out, however, and the depths turn inky black as the shallows drop off along dramatic cliffs, a magnet for experienced divers.

Most people who take to the waters here rest up on the unblemished beaches of the island. But those aching for a walk can visit Bali's oldest temple, **Pura Gili Kencana**, dating from the 14th century.

Dive shops across Bali arrange trips to Menjangan, but spare yourself a long drive by staying in the nearby north coast village of **Pemuteran**. A number of places to stay, ranging from the impossibly posh to the merely charming, surround a small and sandy cove. **Reef Seen Aquatics** (☎ 0362-93001; www.reefseen.com; Pemuteran) is a long-running operation. The owners are active in various schemes to protect Bali's ever-endangered sea turtles.

Serious divers are likely to take a trip with a dive shop, but casual snorkellers can arrange for a tour (US$35 to US$50 for a four-hour trip) from a Pemuteran hotel or the tiny dock at **Labuhan Lalang**, across from Menjangan.

INFORMATION

Location 150km from Kuta
Getting there It's about three hours by car to Labuhan Lalang from South Bali, then a chartered boat ride to the island
Costs Car rental US$30 per day; car with driver US$40 to US$50 per day
When to go Year-round

WEST BALI

West Bali is the sinuous bit of the island that runs in the shadow of the central string of volcanoes. It is also the least-populated part; much of the land is given over to agriculture. Many visitors limit their time in the area to a rushed visit to **Pura Tanah Lot** (adult/child 10,000/5000Rp), the over-subscribed temple about 10km along the beach from Seminyak. This is a mistake: West Bali in many ways is an undiscovered country of hidden temples, beguiling rice terraces and wild shorelines. In fact, you may want to think twice about visiting Pura Tanah Lot at all. Its location on a rock jutting out of the Indian Ocean is photogenic enough, but you may not be able to see the temple through the forest of people. Like some mob of barn-seeking horses, every tourist bus in Bali seems to turn up here for sunset.

Greener than green -- the rice terraces of Jatiluwih

A much more heavenly experience lies up the hill on the cloud-shrouded slopes of **Gunung Batukau**, Bali's second-highest peak (2276m). Here, amid huge and constantly dripping hardwoods, is **Pura Luhur Batukau** (donation 10,000Rp), one of Bali's most important temples. Except for ceremonial days – worthy spectacles themselves – the temple is rarely crowded. Wander the vaguely Japanese-feeling inner courtyard and take in the incense from the seven-roofed *meru* dedicated to Maha Dewa, the mountain's guardian spirit. Take a short walk around to the left to see a small white-water stream. The air vibrates with the tumbling water.

Off the road to the temple you'll be thankful that green is the most restful colour on the eyes, otherwise you'd go blind. The road to **Jatiluwih** rewards with vistas of centuries-old rice terraces that are a shade of green so pure that most others will forever look like drab olive. Get out of your car and set off like a duck across the terraces.

Back on the coast, untouched beaches uncurl in endless succession. At **Medewi** and a few other spots like **Balian Beach**, surfers have staked their claims, but follow almost any road to the sea and you'll find your own private sandy refuge. In fact, take just about any road at random in West Bali and you'll be rewarded with cathedrals of bamboo arching overhead, lush fruit trees growing wild by the road and water rushing through channels linking the omnipresent rice fields.

INFORMATION

Location West Bali begins about 10km northwest of Seminyak and runs for another 120km west

Getting there The sites are reached between 30 minutes' and two hours' drive via the main west road, which crawls with traffic to the Java ferry port

Costs Car rental US$30 per day; car with driver US$40 to US$50 per day

When to go Year-round

>SNAPSHOTS

Bali's cliché depends on who you are. Cold beer and beaches? Spas and boutiques? But Bali defies easy classification – it can be whatever you want it to be. This chapter spotlights Bali's diversity so that you can make it your own.

It's a hard choice, pool or sea, at the Legian Hotel in Seminyak (p46)

ACCOMMODATION

Most people arrange their accommodation before they arrive in Bali. You can: a) get the best deals this way; and b) avoid traipsing around in the heat with your bags, seeking a room at the inn.

High season in Bali is around Christmas and during the Australian school holidays in July and August. At these times you'll find places booked solid without advance planning. Generally with US$100 per night to spend, Bali's world of accommodation will be your oyster. At quiet times, US$60 will get a fine room in a beachside hotel in Legian, with breakfast and pool.

If you want something truly special, it's hard to beat Bali. Some of Southeast Asia's best hotels are here: expect attentive service, oodles of style and those intangible touches that set the best resorts apart. In high season you'll pay dearly, but in low season some top places cost under US$200.

Generally where you stay in Bali will dictate your choices. Although exceptions abound, the following generalisations are a guide. Kuta has cheap accommodation crammed into its narrow lanes, within stumbling distance of raucous nightclubs. Legian is calmer and has good midrange hotels off the beach and some family-oriented resorts along the beach.

Seminyak has some of Bali's best beach resorts. The Oberoi is still a trendsetter more than 30 years after it opened. Villas are big here and to the north. Typically these are small private compounds with plunge pools, open-air living spaces and sometimes a small staff for cooking and chores. Rates range from US$300 a night to 10 times that or more.

South of the airport there are scores of funky little cliffside guesthouses with sweeping views of the surf breaks along the Bukit Peninsula to Ulu

---

lonely planet Hotels & Hostels

Need a place to stay? Find and book it at lonelyplanet.com. Over 50 properties are featured for Bali — each personally visited, thoroughly reviewed and happily recommended by a Lonely Planet author. From hostels to high-end hotels, we've hunted out the places that will bring you unique and special experiences. Read independent reviews by authors and other travellers, and get practical information including amenities, maps and photos. Then reserve your room simply and securely via Hotels & Hostels — our online booking service. It's all at lonelyplanet.com/hotels.

Watu. To the east, Nusa Dua is a cloistered resort area with huge and often bland hotels. Sanur has smaller places with sedate charm overlooking its calm beach and nearby streets. In both the east and the west of Bali you'll find places ranging from modest to opulent dotted along the coasts.

Ubud has a vast range of choices. Exclusive resorts have views of lush river valleys and sinuous rice terraces. Even modest hotels often have an in-house spa. For about US$25 you can have a well-appointed room in any of dozens of traditional family compounds near the centre.

One thing: if you get to Bali and don't like your choice, don't hesitate to go somewhere else. At most times of the year you'll be spoilt for choice.

WEB RESOURCES

AsiaRooms.com www.asiarooms.com
Bali Discovery www.balidiscovery.com
Otel.com www.otel.com

BEST FOR THE BEACH
> Conrad Resort (www.conradhotels.com; Tajung Benoa)
> La Taverna (www.latavernahotel.com; Sanur)
> Pondok Baruna (www.world-diving.com; Nusa Lembongan)
> Samaya (www.thesamayabali.com; Seminyak)
> Tandjung Sari (www.tandjungsari.com; Pemuteran, north coast)

BEST FOR THE BEST
> Amandari (www.amandari.com; Ubud)
> Amankila (www.amanresorts.com; near Manggis, East Bali)
> Four Seasons Jimbaran Bay (www.fourseasons.com; Jimbaran)
> Oberoi (www.oberoihotels.com; Seminyak)
> Sentosa (www.balisentosa.com; Seminyak)

BEST ON A BUDGET
> Artini Cottages (www.artinicottage.com; Ubud)
> Flashbacks (www.flashbacks-chb.com; Sanur)
> Hotel Kumala Pantai (www.kumalapantai.com; Legian)
> Masa Inn (www.masainn.com; Kuta)
> Oka Wati Hotel (www.okawatihotel.com; Ubud)

BEST HIDEAWAYS
> Alam Indah (www.alamindahbali.com; Ubud)
> Hotel Tugu Bali (www.tuguhotels.com; Canggu, Kerobokan)
> Nirarta (www.awareness-bali.com; Sidemen, East Bali)
> Nusa Lembongan Resort (www.nusa-lembongan.com; Nusa Lembongan)
> Puri Lumbung Cottages (www.purilumbung.com; Munduk, central mountains)

FOOD

Compared with other Indonesian islands, Balinese food is more pungent and lively. The biting note of fresh ginger is matched by the heat of raw chillies, shrimp paste, palm sugar and tamarind. There is nothing shy about this cuisine and it is certainly not as sweet and subtle as the food of the neighbouring island of Java.

There are shades of South Indian, Malaysian and Chinese flavours in Balinese food. It has evolved from years of cross-cultural cook-ups and trading with sea-faring pioneers, and perhaps even pirates, across the seas of Asia. The idea that you should only eat what is native to the soil doesn't apply in this part of the world, because even the humble chilli was introduced by the fearless Portuguese, along with a plethora of other colourful, edible exotica from the New World.

For a cuisine that is so nuanced, it may surprise that more often than not it is simply wolfed down. The Western idea of coming together doesn't apply to the Balinese, who eat when they are hungry. Gatherings involving food are saved for ceremonies and festivals. Balinese meals are most often cooked by vendors, whether working a roaring wok, pushing a cart (the ultimate convenience food) or slaving away all morning so that hordes can descend at lunch and lay waste to dozens of warung dishes.

Given the many influences found in a Balinese meal, it's fitting that fusion cooking is the hallmark of inventive menus found from Seminyak to Ubud. In the best Balinese tradition, creative chefs take techniques and influences from across the globe and combine them into menus that surprise and delight. On a list of reasons to visit Bali, the food – from humble to extravagant – must always be there. And don't miss lunch at a warung, where you choose from an array of dishes and then chow down elbow to elbow with other happy diners at communal tables.

BEST BALINESE
> Cak Asm (p87)
> Warung Dobiel (p77)
> Warung Kolega (p61)
> Warung Ibu Oka (p96)

BEST EVER
> Biku (p52)
> Bumbu Bali (p75)
> Sardine (p59)

BEST BUDGET
> Ayam Goreng Kalasan (p87)
> Warung Gossip (p61)
> Warung Italia (p54)
> Warung Sulawesi (p61)

BEST FOR FUN
> Cafe Havana (p95)
> Indo-National (p41)
> Naughty Nuri's (p96)
> Teba Mega Cafe (p65)

Top left A Japanese spread is one of many many eating options **Above** A mobile food stall offers the ultimate convenience

SNAPSHOTS

BARS & CLUBS

'Coldest beer in Bali!' It's an oft-repeated claim and a highly dubious one, since the competition to actually achieve the title would mean your beer came frozen on a stick. Yet there's no denying the appeal of a cold beer during the heat of day or the warmth of night in Bali. It's all the better given that the near-ubiquitous brew, Bintang, is a good, clean-tasting lager that doesn't wear out its welcome after the first, fifth or 50th time.

Where you down your Bintang may also feel near-ubiquitous. Few if any walls, lots of thatching, simple tables and relaxed yet chatty servers easily describes the majority of bars in South Bali. Most places to drink are also places to eat. A few coldies, a hot plate of something, lots of merry chit-chat and, before you know it, an entire evening is gone.

You'll find stylish cocktail lounges mostly at top-end hotels, and even then Bintang prevails. No matter the venue, wine drinkers are better off developing a craving for beer, rum or gin as Bali is not a place for sipping a vintage glass of something clever. Wine lists worthy of the name are few; the local wine is for emergency use only.

However, it's worth noting that a few lounges are appearing that break with the *South Pacific* cliché. Whether in the guise of restaurant-cum-clubs in Seminyak or upmarket venues for the Kuta mobs, the kind of Western boozers that put form before function may be ready to have their day in Bali.

For many, however, Bintangs over an evening are but a prelude to Bali's real nightlife. The nightclubs of Kuta, Legian and Seminyak draw acolytes from across Southeast Asia. The large numbers of relatively well heeled tourists and nonexistent licensing laws have spawned an ever-changing line-up of clubs that book celebrity DJs and list 'am' rather than 'pm' as their closing time. Bouncing from one club to another all night long is a Bali tradition that guarantees you'll be overheated from the exertion, the mixes, the booze, the companionship or all of the above.

BEST AT SUNSET
> Beach House (p60)
> Mano (p54)
> Scooby Doo Cafe (p107)
> Zanzibar (p43)

BEST FOR MEMORY LOSS
> Apache Reggae Bar (p45)
> Bounty (p45)
> Café Billiard (p83)
> Double Six Club (p45)

Top left Your cocktail is waiting to be prepared for you **Above** A cold beer on a warm night, and throw in good company

SHOPPING & MARKETS

A billion beads. That's about how many you can buy from over 100 shops selling the same during a walk from Legian to Seminyak. If at first glance Bali seems to be one big hawker stall (often euphemistically named an 'Art Market') of Bintang T-shirts and Chinese baubles, look further and you'll soon see why so many people leave the island with new suitcases.

In the same way that the cheaper cost of living coupled with high visitor numbers has drawn creative chefs itching to cut their teeth, so too has the shopping scene proven fertile for waves of young designers and artisans, both Balinese and expat. And if it seems you can't run into someone in Seminyak and *not* have them claim to be a designer, the reality is that many actually are. The shopping scene is like a form of primordial soup. New boutiques appear, old ones vanish, some change into something else while others move up the food chain. The odds that you'll stumble onto a star of tomorrow are good.

Despite the inroads of international chains, Bali's traditional markets are still the venue of choice for most shoppers. And they should be, with their beautiful and accessible displays of the best the island has to offer. These shady labyrinths are the connection between the people doing the producing and the people doing the consuming. Drop by to see the makings of temple offerings, exotic fruits and everything you need to whip up a 12-course Balinese feast.

BEST SHOPPING STREETS
> Jl Dewi Sita (Map p89, C4)
> Jl Oberoi (Map p47, C2)
> Jl Raya Seminyak (Map p47, E2, E3, E4)
> Monkey Forest Rd (Map p89, C5)

BEST MARKETS
> Fruit Market (p59)
> Morning Market (p64)
> Pasar Badung (p86)
> Pasar Kumbasari (p86)

HEALTH & WELLBEING

Whether it's a total fix for the mind, body and spirit, or simply the desire for some quick-fix serenity, lots of travellers in Bali are spending hours and days being massaged, scrubbed, perfumed, pampered, bathed and blissed-out. Sometimes this happens on the beach or in a garden; other times you'll find yourself in stylish, even lavish surroundings.

Every upmarket hotel worth its stars has spa facilities (almost always open to nonguests) offering health, beauty and relaxation treatments. Day spas are also common, with many of the best booked up days in advance during high season. The cost can be anything from a 20,000Rp beach rub to a multihour sybaritic soak for US$100 or more. In general, however, the costs are quite low compared with other parts of the world and the Balinese have just the right cultural background and disposition to enhance the serenity.

The Balinese massage techniques of stretching, long strokes, skin rolling and palm and thumb pressure result in a lowering of tension, improved blood flow and circulation, and an all-over feeling of calm. Based on traditional herbal treatments, popular spa options include the *mandi rempah* (spice bath) and the *mandi susu* (milk bath). The *mandi rempah* begins with a massage, followed by a body scrub with a paste made from assorted spices, and ending with a herbal-and-spice hot bath.

Good spas can be found wherever there are tourists. But Ubud and Seminyak have the best range of options, including truly world-class operations that may have you floating home.

Indulge in some spa luxury

SNAPSHOTS

KIDS

Bali is a good place for kids. There's lots of fun and frolic and the locals are especially enamoured of pint-sized visitors. To the Balinese, children are considered part of the community and everyone, not just the parents, has a responsibility towards them. If a child cries, the Balinese get most upset and insist on finding a parent and handing the child over with a reproachful look. Sometimes they despair of uncaring Western parents, and the child will be whisked off to a place where it can be cuddled, cosseted and fed.

Children are a social asset when you travel in Bali, and people will display great interest in any Western child they meet. You will have to learn your child's age and sex in Bahasa Indonesia – *bulau* (month), *tahun* (year), *laki-laki* (boy) and *perempuan* (girl). You should also make polite inquiries about the other person's children, present or absent.

For the kids there's the adventure of a new and very different place. And there are lots of fun things to do, including beaches and pools (almost every hotel has one). In restaurants it's likely that the kitchen will happily knock out a kid-sized spag bol or a burger on demand. And for modest sums, a girl can get her hair plaited and a boy can get a barbed-wire henna tattoo, among other experiences unthinkable at home.

And amid all this chatter about what kids want, let's not forget the adults. Skilled, caring childcare is easily arranged while you go out and play.

BEST FUN
> Bali Safari & Marine Park (p103)
> Elephant Safari Park (p92)
> Pura Luhur Ulu Watu
  (p68)
> Waterbom Park (p39)

BEST PLACE TO LOSE PARENTS
> Rip Curl School of Surf (p39)
> Sacred Monkey Forest Sanctuary
  (p91)
> Surfer Girl (p40)
> Surya Water Sports (p81)

LOST IN BALI

Sitting on Jl Sunset in traffic moving slower than the immigration lines at Ngurah Rai Airport, you may think that a Bali where you can lose yourself is pure fantasy: a Bintang-fuelled vision worthy of a madman. Well, you'd be wrong. Bali may have 3.2 million people crammed into a rambutan-sized island, and it may welcome two million visitors a year, but there are special places where you can not only find solitude but also begin to find your own spiritual link to the island.

How about a long walk on a beach? Go east or go west. From a few kilometres past Sanur until the island turns north, East Bali has countless beaches where it could easily be you, the surf and a bird. The same goes for West Bali. From just west of Pura Tanah Lot, the sand just keeps going.

Although Ubud is always popular, it's simple to lose the pack: just start walking. Like other places in Bali such as Sidemen Rd, there are scores of walks out into the verdant countryside. Within 15 minutes of leaving central Ubud, you'll be as solitary as a duck in a rice field that made a wrong turn on the way to the snail festival.

Or just get up early. Dawn over the beach in Kuta or Seminyak is just as magical – and uncrowded – as the loneliest beach further afield.

Discover natural wonders in Bali

GAY BALI

Bali easily ranks as one of the most tolerant places gay people can visit. Much of this stems from the beliefs and attitudes ingrained in the Balinese. People are accepted as they are, judging others is considered extremely rude and as there's a very limited macho culture, masculinity is not easily threatened.

Homosexuality among visitors has a long tradition on the island. Many of the island's most influential expatriate artists have been more-or-less openly gay. One need only look at the art of Antonio Blanco in Ubud to understand that a certain amount of flamboyance is considered a bonus.

Many Balinese openly become involved with visitors of the same sex, although this is far more common with men than with women. There is no thought given to possible social ramifications among their friends, family or neighbours. In fact, Bali is something of a haven for gay people from across Indonesia.

One of the converse effects about having gay life so much a part of life in Bali is that there are relatively few 'gay' places. The default is that almost everywhere is mixed since sexual orientation is not something that is judged. However, that doesn't mean there aren't plenty of gay cliques, especially in Seminyak, which actually has no shortage of cliques of every kind. Spa Bonita in Kerobokan and Q-Bar are almost community centres.

Finally, homosexual behaviour is not illegal in Bali and the age of consent for sexual activity is 16 years. Gay men in Indonesia are referred to as *homo* or *gay* and are quite distinct from the female impersonators called *waria*. *Lesbian* is also the term for gay women in Bali.

>BACKGROUND

Traditional Bali Aga dancer from Tenganan (p103)

BACKGROUND

HISTORY

There are few traces of Stone Age people in Bali, although it's certain that the island was populated very early in prehistoric times – fossilised humanoid remains from neighbouring Java have been dated from as early as 250,000 years ago. Artefacts indicate that the Bronze Age began in Bali before 300 BC.

Little is known of Bali during the period when Indian traders brought Hinduism to the Indonesian archipelago, although it is thought it was embraced on the island by the 7th century AD. By the 9th century Bali had already developed many similarities to the island you find today. Rice, for example, was grown with the help of a complex irrigation system, probably very like that employed now, and the Balinese had also begun to develop their rich cultural and artistic traditions.

Java began to spread its influence into Bali during the reign of King Airlangga (1019–42), or perhaps even earlier. At the age of 16, when his uncle lost the throne, Airlangga fled into the forests of western Java. He gradually gained support, won back the kingdom and went on to become one of Java's greatest kings. Airlangga's mother had moved to Bali and remarried shortly after his birth, so when he gained the throne there was an immediate link between Java and Bali.

After Airlangga's death, Bali remained mostly semi-independent. Meanwhile, as several Hindu states fell and Islam gained traction across the archipelago, many of the intelligentsia fled to Bali. Notable among these was the 15th-century priest Nirartha, who is credited with introducing many of the complexities of Balinese religion to the island, as well as

DYING FOR FREEDOM

During the Dutch military campaign across South Bali from 1906 to 1908, thousands of Balinese – led by priests and royalty – chose certain death in battle over capitulation. During suicidal *puputans* (a warrior's fight to the death), the princes burned their palaces, and then, dressed in their finest jewellery and waving ceremonial golden kris (daggers), marched out to face the modern weapons of the Dutch. During several of these spectacles the Dutch implored the Balinese to surrender rather than make their hopeless stand, but their pleas went unheeded. The last *puputan* took place in 1908 at Semarapura; the beautiful ruins there are all that remains of the palace.

KUTA'S FIRST TOURISTS

Robert Koke and Louise Garret, an American couple, landed in Bali in 1936 as part of a global adventure. Horrified at the stuffy strictures imposed by the Dutch tourism authorities, the pair built a couple of bungalows out of palm leaves and other local materials on the otherwise deserted beach at Kuta.

Word soon spread and the Kokes were booked solid. Guests came for days, stayed for weeks and told their friends. Other Westerners built their own thatched hotels, complete with the bungalows that were to become a Balinese cliché in the decades ahead.

The war ended tourism but in the 1950s small thatched bungalows again began appearing on the beach at Kuta. Besides helping start modern tourism in Bali, Robert Koke left another lasting impression: he taught local boys to surf.

establishing the chain of 'sea temples' that includes Pura Luhur Ulu Watu (p68) and Pura Tanah Lot (p114).

The first Europeans to set foot in Bali itself were Dutch seamen in 1597. At that time, Balinese prosperity and artistic activity, at least among the royalty, was at a peak, and the king who befriended explorer Cornelis de Houtman had 200 wives and a chariot pulled by two white buffaloes, not to mention a retinue of 50 dwarfs whose bodies had been bent to resemble the handle of a kris (traditional dagger). By the early 1600s the Dutch had established trade treaties with Javanese princes and controlled much of the spice trade, but they were interested in profit, not culture, and barely gave Bali a second glance.

By the 18th century, bickering amongst various Balinese princes caused the island's power structure to fragment. In 1846 the Dutch landed military forces in northern Bali. Focus turned to the south and in 1906 Dutch warships appeared at Sanur.

The Dutch forces landed despite Balinese opposition and had complete control of the island by 1908. Many thousands of Balinese – including royalty and priests – chose suicide in battle rather than occupation (see boxed text, opposite). Although under Dutch control and part of the Dutch East Indies, there was little development in Bali, and the common people noticed little difference between Dutch and royal rule.

The Japanese occupied Bali in 1942 and conditions during WWII were grim. In August 1945, just days after the Japanese surrender, Soekarno, a prominent nationalist, proclaimed Indonesia's independence. Battles raged in Bali and elsewhere until the Dutch gave up and recognised Indonesia's independence in 1949, with President Soekarno as leader.

Independence was not easy for Indonesia. In Bali, there were sharp differences between traditionalists, who wanted to maintain the old caste system, and radicals, who saw the caste system as repressive and championed land reform. After a failed coup in Jakarta in 1965, religious traditionalists in Bali led a witch-hunt for 'godless communists'. Before the slaughter was over, an estimated 50,000 to 100,000 people out of a population of about two million were killed.

General Soeharto played a major role in suppressing the coup and soon assumed the presidency, leading his Golkar party to easy election wins until 1999. This period was also marked by great economic development in Bali, which brought great riches to the ruling elite. Projects like the tourist enclave of Nusa Dua date from this era.

In early 1997 the Indonesian currency (the rupiah) all but collapsed due to Southeast Asia's economic crisis. Trying to cope, Soeharto agreed to economic reforms that cut subsidies for food and fuel. Riots broke out across Indonesia and Soeharto eventually resigned. In 1999 Indonesia's parliament met to elect a new president. The front-runner was Megawati Sukarnoputri, whose party received the largest number of votes at the election. Megawati was enormously popular in Bali, partly because of family connections (her paternal grandmother was Balinese) and partly because her party was essentially secular (the mostly Hindu Balinese are very concerned about any growth in Muslim fundamentalism). However, through shrewd politicking Abdurrahman Wahid, the moderate, intellectual head of Indonesia's largest Muslim organisation, emerged as president, with Megawati as vice president.

As with Soekarno, Wahid's moral stature and vast intellect did not translate into administrative competence. After 21 months of growing ethnic, religious and regional conflicts, parliament recalled Wahid and handed the presidency to Megawati.

Indonesia's cultural wars continued and certainly played a role in the October 2002 bombings in Kuta. More than 200 tourists and Balinese were killed and hundreds more were injured. Tourism immediately fell by more than half.

The elections of 2004 were remarkably peaceful. Susilo Bambang Yudhoyono (popularly known as 'SBY') won and continues as president after easily winning re-election in 2009. The former general has been put to the test numerous times by calamities such as the 2004 tsunami that devastated Aceh.

Meanwhile, Bali is on a roll. The hero of the 2002 bombing investigations, Made Pastika, is governor and he has brought focus on the island's many challenges, such as its gravely threatened environment. Over two million visitors a year turn up and development is everywhere. People are starting to ask: 'can we be too popular?'

LIFE IN BALI

Balinese life centres on the village, and, increasingly, the suburban neighbourhoods of the south. Every activity – producing crops, preparing food, bargaining with tourists, keeping their youth employed – involves everybody, making it impossible to be a faceless nonentity on the island. This involvement with the other people in their village extends to the tourists. To make you feel welcome, Balinese will go out of their way to chat to you. But they won't talk about the weather or even the football. They are interested in you, your home life and your personal relationships. Chatting in Bali can get rather surprisingly intimate. ('How many children do you have' is just a start.)

AVOIDING OFFENCE

Although the Balinese are pretty darn mellow, be aware and respectful of local sensibilities, and dress and act appropriately. When in doubt let the words modest and humble guide you.

> An increasing number of younger Balinese now adopt the dress of visitors, which means you'll see shorts everywhere. But overly revealing clothing is still frowned upon – few want to see your butt crack.
> While many women go topless on Bali's tourist beaches, locals inwardly shudder at this.
> Take off your shoes before entering a mosque or someone's house.
> Don't touch anyone on the head, as it is regarded as the abode of the soul and is therefore sacred.
> Pass things with your right hand.

Temple Etiquette

Foreigners can enter most temple complexes if properly dressed. In most cases, an acceptable show of respect for the gods is clean, tidy clothing and a *selandong* (traditional scarf) or sash to tie around your waist – some temples have these for hire (around 2000Rp or a donation).

Usually there's a sign at temple entrances warning you to be respectful, and asking that women don't enter if menstruating. At this time women are thought to be *sebel* (ritually unclean), as are pregnant women and those who have recently given birth, or been recently bereaved.

For the average rural Balinese, the working day is not long. Their expertise at coaxing bountiful harvests from the fertile volcanic soil leaves them free for lots of quality time to chat or prepare elaborate cultural events.

In the more urbanised south, however, life embodies many of the same hassles of modern life anywhere. There's traffic and noise that drowns out even the loudest barking dog, plus various social ills such as drugs and the like. Still there is a concept of village life under it all, in that people are part of a greater group beyond their immediate family. These days an air-conditioned mall fills in for the village banyan tree as a meeting place for many.

Women enjoy a prominent position in Bali, and can be seen in everything from manual labour jobs – you'll see them carrying baskets of wet cement on their heads – to almost every job in the tourist industry. In fact the traditional female role of caring for people and preparing food means that many successful tourist shops and cafes have been established by women.

RELIGION

Traditional Balinese society is founded on the Balinese Hindu religion and it permeates every aspect of life. There are temples in every village, shrines in every field, and offerings are made at every corner, nook and cranny. Major temples come to life at regular and colourful temple festivals that involve lavish communal offerings and processions.

Hinduism is practised by more than 90% of islanders. The Balinese overlaid the Majapahit interpretation of Hinduism on their animist beliefs – hence the unique local form of the religion. Balinese worship the trinity

OFFERINGS

Balinese believe that the island is populated with gods, ancestors, spirits and demons. Offerings are presented all through the day to show respect and gratitude, and each is a small work of art. Once presented to the gods, an offering cannot be used again, so new offerings are made again and again each day, usually by women (as more women hold jobs, you'll see easy-to-assemble offerings for sale in markets – much as you'll find quick dinner items in Western supermarkets). Offerings come in many forms although typically they are little bigger than a guidebook. Expect to see flowers and bits of food – especially rice – presented on a leaf. More important shrines and occasions draw far more elaborate creations.

of Brahma, Shiva and Vishnu, three aspects of the one god, Sanghyang Widi. The basic threesome is always alluded to but never seen – a vacant shrine or empty throne tells all.

Islam is a minority religion in Bali, comprising less than 10% of the population. Some are descendants of seafaring people from Sulawesi while many others are Javanese drawn by economic opportunity.

ARTS

The richness of Bali's arts and crafts has its origin in the fertility of the land. The purest forms are the depictions of Dewi Sri, the rice goddess, intricately made from dried and folded strips of palm leaf to ensure that the fertility of the rice fields continues.

Until the tourist invasion, the acts of painting or carving were purely to decorate temples and shrines as well as enrich ceremonies. Today, with galleries and craft shops everywhere, paintings are stacked up on gallery floors and you may trip over carvings from both stone and wood. Much of this work is churned out quickly, but you will still find a great deal of beautiful work. Today you can still enjoy Bali's renowned dance, which is accompanied by its unique and lyrical gamelan music. And anywhere there are tourists you'll see examples of painting and other arts and crafts.

DANCE

You can catch a quality dance performance in Bali anywhere there's a festival or celebration. Enjoying this purely Balinese form of art is reason enough to visit, and no visit is complete without this quintessential Bali experience.

Balinese love a blend of seriousness and slapstick, and this shows in their dances. Some have a decidedly comic element, with clowns who convey the story and also act as a counterpoint to the staid, noble characters. Most dancers are not professionals. Dance is learned by performing, and by carefully following the movements of an expert. It tends to be precise, jerky, shifting and jumpy, remarkably like Balinese music. Every movement of wrist, hand and fingers is charged with meaning, while facial expressions are carefully choreographed to convey the character of the dance.

Probably the best known of the dances is the Kecak, which tells a tale from the *Ramayana*, one of the great Hindu holy books, about Prince Rama and Princess Sita. Throughout performances the dancing and chanting are superbly synchronised with an eerily exciting coordination. Add in actors posing as an army of monkeys and you have an unbeatable spectacle.

Another popular dance for tourists shows a battle between good (the Barong) and bad (the Rangda). The Barong is a strange but good, mischievous and fun-loving shaggy dog-lion. The widow-witch Rangda is bad through and through.

The most graceful of Balinese dances, Legong, is performed by young girls. It is so important in Balinese culture that in old age a classic dancer will be remembered as a 'great legong'.

You'll find exceptional dance performances in and around Ubud. Many tourist shows in South Bali hotels offer a smorgasbord of dances – a little Kecak, a taste of Legong and some Barong to round it off. Some of these performances can be pretty abbreviated with just a few musicians and a couple of dancers.

MUSIC

Balinese music is based around an ensemble known as a gamelan, also called a *gong*. A *gong gede* (large orchestra) is the traditional form, with 35 to 40 musicians. The *gong kebyar* is the modern, popular form, and has up to 25 instruments. Although it sounds strange at first with its noisy, jangly percussion, it's exciting, enjoyable, melodic and at times haunting. Gamelan is a part of most dance performances.

PAINTING

Balinese painting is probably the art form most influenced by Western ideas and demand. There's a relatively small number of creative original painters, and an enormous number of imitators. Originality is not considered as important in Bali as it is in the West. Even some renowned artists will simply draw the design, decide the colours and leave apprentices to apply the paint. Thus, shops are packed full of paintings in the popular styles – some of them are quite good. It's rare to see anything totally new.

Traditional paintings faithfully depicting religious and mythological symbolism were customarily for temple and palace decoration. After the 1930s Western artists introduced the novel concept that paintings could also be artistic creations that could be sold for money. The range of themes, techniques, styles and materials expanded enormously.

Ubud's art museums (p90) have a broad range of beautiful paintings by both Balinese and influential Westerners like Walter Spies and Arie Smit. Styles range from abstract works of incredible colour to beautiful and evocative representations – some highly idealised – of island life. The Belgian painter Le Mayeur set the standard for this at his home in Sanur (p80).

CRAFTS

Bali is a showroom for all the crafts of Indonesia. A stylish boutique or shop will sell batik from Java, ikat garments from Sumba, Sumbawa and Flores, as well as textiles and woodcarvings from Bali, Lombok and Kalimantan.

Carving was traditionally done for temples and the Balinese are experts. These days the emphasis is on what sells (although there's always something special), the technical skill is high and the Balinese sense of humour shines through – like a frog clutching a leaf as an umbrella, or a weird demon on the side of a bell clasping his hands over his ears.

Masks are a popular purchase. The mask maker must know the movements that each performer uses, so that the character can be shown by the mask. The results are both dramatic and colourful.

Stone carving appears in set places in temples. Door guardians are usually a protective personality like Arjuna. Above the main entrance, Kala's monstrous face often peers out, his hands reaching out beside his head to catch any evil spirits. The side walls of a *pura dalem* (temple of the dead) might feature sculpted panels that show the horrors that await evildoers in the afterlife. Batubulan, on the main highway from South Bali to Ubud, is a major stone-carving centre. Stone figures 25cm to 2m in height line both sides of the road, and stone carvers can be seen in action in the many workshops.

GOVERNMENT & ECONOMY

Bali's 3.2 million people mostly live in the south, mostly in the Badung province or its offshoot, Denpasar. Like the seven other districts, Badung mostly follows the old regency boundaries of the royal era. Governors are elected and act as middlemen between Jakarta and Bali. Their power over the individual districts is open for debate.

Within Bali's government the most important body is also the most local. More than 3500 neighbourhood organisations called *banjar* wield enormous power. Comprising the married men of a given area (some-where between 50 and 500), a *banjar* controls most community activities, whether it's planning for a temple ceremony or making important land-use decisions. Decisions are reached by consensus.

Although women and even children can belong to the *banjar,* only men attend the meetings. Women, who often own the businesses in tourist areas, have to communicate through their husbands to be able to exert their influence. One thing that outsiders in a neighbourhood quickly learn is that it does not pay to cross the *banjar*. Entire streets of restaurants and bars in Seminyak have been closed by order of the *banjar* after its expressed concerns over matters such as noise were not respected.

Tourism is the engine of Balinese economic life. It accounts for about 50% of the economy and provides the bulk of the jobs. It also draws in huge investment from outside Bali. Tourism numbers are topping two million annually with each year setting a new record. Coffee, copra, seaweed and cattle are major agricultural exports – most of the rice goes to feed Bali's own population.

ENVIRONMENT

Bali is a small island, midway along the string of islands that makes up the Indonesian archipelago. It's adjacent to the most heavily populated island of Java, and immediately west of the chain of smaller islands comprising Nusa Tenggara.

The island is visually dramatic. A mountainous chain with a string of active volcanoes, it includes several peaks around 2000m. Gunung Agung, the 'Mother Mountain', is over 3000m high. The agricultural lands are south and north of the central mountains. The southern region is a wide, gently sloping area, where most of the country's abundant rice crop is grown. The northern coastal strip is narrower, rising rapidly into the foothills of the central range. It receives less rain but coffee, copra, rice and cattle are farmed here.

Bali's wildlife has been driven out by the dense population, although lizards are common. Rodents too. And monkeys; irritating monkeys.

Offshore matters are different. There is a rich variety of coral, seaweed, fish and other marine life in the coastal waters. Much of it can be appreci-ated by snorkellers, but the larger marine animals are only likely to be seen while diving.

SUSTAINABLE TRAVEL IN BALI

Visitors trying to lessen their impact on Bali should think in terms of less. Walk instead of taking a taxi, say no to plastic bags in the store, ask your hotel if you can refill your water bottles (and if the answer is no, ask why), order locally sourced food and just generally keep this in mind: 'do I need to expend those resources?'

Although purely natural areas are limited by land-use pressures (not that we're complaining about the beautiful rice terraces), Balinese gardens are a delight. The soil and climate can support a huge range of plants, and the Balinese love of beauty and the abundance of cheap labour means that every space can be landscaped.

ENVIRONMENTAL CONCERNS

A fast-growing population in Bali has put pressure on limited resources. The tourist industry has attracted new residents from places like Java and today's rice field is tomorrow's villa or shopping mall.

Water use is a major concern; something unthinkable a few years ago on an island that flows with water. Typical top-end hotels use more than 500L of water a day per room and the growing number of golf courses suck an already stressed resource. At the other end, water pollution is a problem and the recent start of a new sewer system in the south is barely a finger in the dyke. The vast mangroves along the south coast near Benoa Harbour are losing their ability to filter the water that drains here from much of the island.

Air pollution is yet another problem as anyone stuck behind a smoke-belching truck or bus on the traffic-clogged roads knows. And it's not just all those plastic bags and water bottles but the sheer volume of waste produced by the ever-growing population that is another problem. What to do with it? So far answers to these problems have been deferred.

FURTHER READING

Eat, Pray, Love (known to wags locally as 'that damn book') is the enormous best-seller (and movie starring Julia Roberts) that has attracted many a Western woman to Bali to find the answer to life's dreams. Author Elizabeth Gilbert ends up in Bali where she makes witty observations about local life, does much histrionic emoting and finds her own answer to everything: a Brazilian husband.

Diana Darling's *The Painted Alphabet* is based on a Balinese epic poem with all the usual ingredients: good, evil, a quest, baby swapping and various mystical events. It's a gentle and beguiling way to get your head into Balinese folklore.

A House in Bali by Colin McPhee is the timeless classic about a Canadian who experienced Bali cultural and village life to the core in the 1930s.

Our Hotel in Bali by Louise Koke is another classic about Westerners in Bali in the 1930s. She and her husband Bob created the first-ever Kuta Beach hotel and had numerous delightful encounters along the way. It's a quick and fun read with lots of photos.

Gecko's Complaint is a morality tale presented as an old Balinese children's fable. The recent Periplus edition is richly illustrated.

DIRECTORY
TRANSPORT
ARRIVAL & DEPARTURE
AIR

The only airport in Bali, Ngurah Rai Airport (DPS) is just south of Kuta, but it's sometimes referred to internationally as Denpasar, or on some internet flight booking sites as Bali.

The **international terminal** (Map p63, B1; ☎ 0361-751011) and **domestic terminal** (☎ 0361-751011) are a few hundred metres apart. Immigration lines in the former can be notoriously long (two-plus hours). From the official counters, just outside the terminals, there are usually hassle-free prepaid airport taxis. Ignore any touts that aren't part of the official scheme. The costs (depending on drop-off point):

Destination	Cost
Denpasar	85,000Rp
Jimbaran	60,000Rp
Kuta Beach	50,000Rp
Legian	55,000Rp
Nusa Dua	95,000Rp
Sanur	95,000Rp
Seminyak	70,000Rp
Ubud	195,000Rp

If you have a surfboard, you'll be charged at least 35,000Rp extra, depending on its size. Many hotels will offer to pick you up at the airport, but there's no need to use this service if it costs more than the above rates.

The thrifty can walk across the airport car park to the right (northeast) from the international and domestic terminals and continue a couple of hundred metres through the vehicle exit to the airport road (ignoring any touts along the way), where you can hail a Bali Taxi for about half the above amounts.

VISA

The visa situation in Indonesia seems to be constantly in flux. It is essential that you confirm current formalities before you arrive in Bali. No matter what type of visa you are going to use, your passport *must* be valid for at least six months from the date of your arrival.

The main visa options for visitors to Bali:

Visa in Advance Citizens of countries not eligible for Visa Free or Visa on Arrival must apply for a visa before they arrive in Indonesia. Typically this is a visitors' visa, which comes in two flavours: 30 or 60 days. Details vary by country, so you should contact the nearest Indonesian embassy or consulate for details.

Visa on Arrival Citizens of over 50 countries may apply for a 30-day visa when they arrive at the airport in Bali. The cost is US$25, collectable on the spot, and it is best to have this in the exact amount in US currency (otherwise the exchange and change process can be both opaque and tedious). You can renew this visa for another 30 days at the often-crowded immigration offices in Bali. Penalties for an expired visa can be severe. Eligible countries include Australia, Austria, Belgium, Canada, Denmark, France, Germany, Ireland, Italy, Japan, the Netherlands, New Zealand, Russia, South Africa, Spain, Switzerland, Sweden, Taiwan, UK and USA.

Visa Free Citizens of Singapore and a smattering of other countries can receive a nonextendable 30-day visa for free upon arrival.

DEPARTURE TAX
The airport departure tax from Bali is 40,000Rp (domestic) and 150,000Rp (international). Have exact cash for the booths located right before passport control as you are leaving.

GETTING AROUND
Traffic aside, Bali is not a large island (approximately 100km by 160km) and roads are good. You can drive all the way around it in a day. How you do so is the question. Roads are chaotic and trying to navigate them driving a hired car may take the holiday out of your vacation (although many people do drive, it's just not relaxing). The solution is to let someone else do the driving. Within minutes of arriving in Bali you'll grow weary of the refrain 'Transport?' from hawkers. Avoid these guys as virtually every place to stay can set you up with a dependable driver for a negotiable US$50 to US$60. You enjoy the sights, the driver honks the horn. For shorter distances, taxis (note, the *right* taxis, see Taxi opposite) are the option of choice for most people.

Public transport is limited to *bemos*, small vans packed with people that run on fixed routes. They are dirt cheap but also uncomfortable and service hours can be erratic. That's one of the reasons every Balinese owns a motorbike.

CLIMATE CHANGE & TRAVEL
Travel – especially air travel – is a significant contributor to global climate change. At Lonely Planet, we believe that all who travel have a responsibility to limit their personal impact. As a result, we have teamed with Rough Guides and other concerned industry partners to support Climate Care, which allows people to offset the greenhouse gases they are responsible for with contributions to energy-saving projects and other climate-friendly initiatives in the developing world. Lonely Planet offsets all staff and author travel.

For more information, turn to the responsible travel pages on www.lonelyplanet.com. For details on offsetting your carbon emissions and a carbon calculator, go to www.climatecare.org.

And remember, it is only 15 minutes' walk along the beach from Kuta to Seminyak.

TAXI

Metered taxis are common in South Bali and Denpasar. They are essential for getting around Kuta and Seminyak, where you can easily flag one down. Elsewhere, they're often a lot less hassle than haggling with drivers.

The usual rate for a taxi is 5000Rp flag fall and 4000Rp per kilometre, but the rate is higher in the evening. If you phone for a taxi, the minimum charge is 10,000Rp. Any driver that claims meter problems or who won't use it should be avoided.

By an order of magnitude, the most reputable taxi agency is **Bali Taxi** (☎ 0361-701111), which uses distinctive blue vehicles bearing the phone number and a bird logo. Drivers speak reasonable English, won't offer you illicit opportunities and will use the meter at all times. There's even

a number to call with **complaints** (☎ 0361-701621).

After Bali Taxi, standards decline rapidly. Some other firms are acceptable, although you may have a hassle getting the driver to use the meter. Negotiated fees can be over the odds; we've heard of cases of 10 times the metered amount.

PRACTICALITIES
BUSINESS HOURS

Government office hours in Bali are roughly from 8am to 3pm Monday to Thursday and from 8am to noon on Friday, but they are not completely standardised. Banking hours are generally from 8am to 2pm Monday to Thursday, from 8am to noon Friday and from 8am to about 11am Saturday. The banks enjoy many public holidays.

In this book it is assumed that restaurants and cafes are usually open about 8am to 10pm daily. Shops and services catering to tourists are open from 9am to about 7pm. Where the hours vary from these, they are noted in the text.

ELECTRICITY

Electricity is usually 220V to 240V AC. Wall plugs are the standard European variety – round with two pins. Service is usually reliable and shops have plug converters.

EMERGENCIES

It's important to note that compared with many places in the world, Bali is fairly safe. There are some hassles from the avaricious, but most visitors face many more dangers at home. Petty theft occurs but it is not prevalent.

Security concerns increased after the 2002 and 2005 bombings but these have tended to fade over time. The odds you will be caught up in such a tragedy are low.

Many visitors regard the persistent attentions of people trying to sell as *the* number-one annoyance in Bali. Around many tourist attractions, visitors are frequently, and often constantly, hassled to buy things. The best way to deal with hawkers is to completely ignore them from the first instance. Eye contact is crucial – don't make any! And don't say anything. A polite 'no thank you' is seen as encouragement. Finally, don't exchange money with people standing on the street. Duh.

Clinics and pharmacies (selling many prescription medicines over the counter) abound in tourist areas. For serious illnesses, **BIMC** (☎ 0361-761263; www.bimcbali.com; Jl Ngurah Rai 100X; ☼ 24hr) is on the bypass road just east of Kuta near the Bali Galleria and easily accessible from most of southern Bali. It's the most modern clinic in Bali and it can arrange medical evacuation.

Ambulance ☎ 118
Police ☎ 110

HOLIDAYS

Bali has a lot of holidays. In addition there are scores more associated with regions and temples. It's worth noting when Nyepi, the Day of Silence, falls each year (see boxed text, p24).

Tahun Baru Masehi (New Year's Day) 1 January
Idul Adha (Muslim festival of sacrifice) February
Muharram (Islamic New Year) February/March
Nyepi (Hindu New Year) March/April
Hari Paskah (Good Friday) April
Ascension of Christ April/May
Hari Waisak (Buddha's birth, enlightenment and death) April/May
Maulud Nabi Mohammed/Hari Natal (Prophet Mohammed's birthday) May
Hari Proklamasi Kemerdekaan (Indonesian Independence Day) 17 August
Isra Miraj Nabi Mohammed (Ascension of the Prophet Mohammed) September
Idul Fitri (End of Ramadan) November/December
Hari Natal (Christmas Day) 25 December

INTERNET

Wi-fi is common in Bali at stylish cafes and bars and in many hotels. Cheap, simple internet access places are common. Often they have computers you may remember from grammar school.

MENU DECODER

Learn just a few words and you'll easily master any local menu, although most places have menus in English.

air botol, **aqua** – bottled water

air minum – drinking water

arak – spirits distilled from palm sap or rice

ayam – chicken

babi – pork

babi guling – spit-roast pig

bakmi – fried noodles

bakso ayam – soup with chicken meatballs

daging sapi – beef

gado-gado – vegetables with peanut sauce

goreng – fry or deep-fry

ikan – fish

kacang tanah – peanut

kare – curry

krupuk udang – prawn crackers

mie goreng – fried noodles with vegetables

nasi campur – plate lunch with rice

nasi goreng – fried rice

nasi putih – plain white steamed rice

pisang goreng – fried banana fritters

rendang – dry beef coconut curry

rijsttafel – literally 'rice table' in Dutch; Indonesian banquet encompassing a selection of spicy meats, fruits, vegetables and sauces served with rice

sambal – chilli sauce

sate – grilled meat on skewers; also satay

soto ayam – light chicken soup

Some sites you may enjoy before arriving:

Bali Advertiser (www.baliadvertiser.biz) This online edition of Bali's expat journal is filled with insider tips.

Bali Discovery (www.balidiscovery.com) Although run by a tour company, this site is easily the best source for Bali news and features, week in and week out. Excellent.

Stranger in Paradise (www.strangerinparadise.com) The online journal of the irrepressible Made Wijaya is filled with insightful and at times hilariously profane takes on local life.

....

MONEY

Indonesia's unit of currency is the rupiah (Rp). There are coins worth 50, 100, 500 and 1000Rp. Notes come in denominations of 500Rp (rare), 1000Rp, 5000Rp, 10,000Rp, 20,000Rp, 50,000Rp and 100,000Rp. Many higher-end establishments quote prices in US dollars (US$). ATMs are common in South Bali, Ubud and most other tourist areas.

You can have a budget surfer holiday with plenty of beer, a US$10 room with fan and cheap meals, and not spend more than $30 a day. Conversely, some of the world's most luxurious hotels are here so there is no ceiling to what you might spend.

Realistically, expect to pay US$50 to US$150 per night for a comfortable air-con room in a nice hotel, depending on the season. Meals are affordable and you can have

BARGAINING

Many everyday purchases in Bali require bargaining. You first establish a starting price – it's usually better to ask the seller for their price rather than make an initial offer. It also helps if you have some idea what the item is worth.

Your first offer can be from one-third to two-thirds of the asking price – assuming that the asking price is not insane. Then, with offer and counteroffer, you'll move closer to an acceptable price someplace in the middle. If you don't get to an acceptable price you can walk away – the vendor often will relent.

But when you name a price, you're committed – you have to buy if your offer is accepted. Throughout the process, good humour is essential.

memorable meals for under US$30. Add another US$20 for entrance fees or cultural tickets, plus transport that averages US$60 for a full day of road-tripping, and you can live well for no more than US$220 a day – and often for around US$100 a day (in low season).

NEWSPAPERS & MAGAZINES

The *International Herald Tribune* is printed in Bali and widely available. Hawkers have copies of Australian dailies for inflated prices that would have Rupert Murdoch drooling. Magazines are limited to major titles.

ORGANISED TOURS

Bali Discovery Tours (☎ 0361-286283; www.balidiscovery.com) Offers numerous and customisable tours that differ from the norm. One visits a small rice-growing village in the west near Tabanan for hands-on demonstrations of cultivation.

JED (Village Ecotourism Network; ☎ 0361-737447; www.jed.or.id) Organises highly regarded tours of small villages, including coffee-growing Pelaga in the mountains, fruit-growing Sibetan in the east, seaweed farms on Nusa Ceningan and ancient Tenganan. You can make arrangements to stay with a family in the villages.

Ubud Tourist Information (p98) It organises simple yet effective cultural tours, especially around special ceremonial events like cremations.

TELEPHONE

The cellular service in Indonesia is GSM. There are several local providers. If your phone company offers international roaming in Indonesia, you can use your own mobile telephone in Bali – check rates with your company.

Alternatively, a GSM mobile phone can be used pretty cheaply if you purchase a prepaid SIM card in Bali. This will cost about 50,000Rp from shops in South Bali and will give you your own local telephone number. However, make certain your phone is both unlocked and able to take SIM cards. Basic phones bought locally start at US$30.

TIPPING

Tipping a set percentage is not expected in Bali, but restaurant workers are poorly paid; if the service is good, it's appropriate to leave 4000Rp or more. Most mid-range hotels and restaurants and all top-end hotels and restaurants add 21% to the bill for tax and service (known as 'plus plus'). This service component is distributed among hotel staff (one hopes), so you needn't tip under these circumstances.

It's also a nice thing to tip taxi drivers, guides, people giving you a massage, those fetching you a beer on the beach etc.

TOURIST INFORMATION

At the time of research, the only true tourist information place was Ubud Tourist Information (see boxed text, p98). Other businesses using this title were travel agents or timeshare condo operations.

TRAVELLERS WITH DISABILITIES

Bali can be hard on those with a disability; even able-bodied people often find it a challenge. There are many pavement hazards and no local laws requiring wheelchair accessibility, never mind specialised services and facilities for those with more complex needs. For people with limited mobility, accommodation options are best at larger hotels. Always check with them personally to see what facilities they have.

>INDEX

See also separate subindexes for See (p157), Do (p158), Shop (p158), Eat (p159), Drink (p159) and Play (p160).

000 map pages

000 map pages